'Popular' Movements and 'Middle Class' Leadership in Late Colonial India

'Popular' Movements and 'Middle Class' Leadership in Late Colonial India

Perspectives and Problems of a "History from Below"

Sumit Sarkar

AAKAR

'Popular' Movements and 'Middle Class' Leadership in Late Colonial India: Perspectives and Problems of a "History from Below"
Sunit Sarkar

First Published 1983
Republished by Aakar 2015
Reprinted 2017

ISBN 978-93-5002-320-4

Published by
AAKAR BOOKS
28 E Pocket IV, Mayur Vihar Phase I
Delhi 110 091, India
aakarbooks@gmail.com
www.aakarbooks.com

Printed at
Sapra Brother, Delhi 110 092

Contents

1

Introduction

A major shift has been taking place in recent years in the historiography of the Indian national movement (perhaps the most rapidly developing sector of modern Indian history writing) through the emergence of a kind of 'history from below'. The new focus is on popular and particularly peasant initiative and 'self mobilization', as distinct from the earlier concentration on national or regional leaders, patriotic ideologies, elite pressures or factional manoeuvres by patron-client linkages. To the practitioners of what some have started calling 'subaltern studies',[1] conventional' nationalist hagiography, Cambridge-type Namierism, and even much of existing Marxist scholarship focussed on party or trade union programmes and organisation appear tainted with various forms of 'elitism'. The transformation being sought for is potentially as significant as those brought about by Lefebvre, Soboul, Rude and Cobb in the historiography of the French Revolution; by Hill (particularly in his later works) and Brian Manning on seventeenth-century England; by Thompson and Gutman in British and American labour history; by Hobsbawm, Rude and Thompson in studies of pre-industrial protest. What we see today are the beginnings of an Indian participation in a worldwide historiographical trend, associated with imaginative use of a wider range of sources, along with a certain distrust, or cynicism about more-or-less bureaucratically-organized and outwardly successful political movements.[2]

'Histories from below' naturally begin by concentrating on local or regional developments, but perhaps the time has come for some tentative generalizations. The first aim of this paper is to bring together the data scattered in a fairly large number of specific studies[3] into some kind of analytical framework, distinguishing various types of 'popular' initiative and 'middle class' response in the pre-Gandhian and Gandhian phases of modern Indian nationalism: I am deliberately using the vague term 'popular', to serve as a convenient shorthand for tribal, peasant, artisan or labour protest, and also because more precise class-analysis is necessarily often difficult in a predominantly pre-industrial society. The category of 'peasant' is, after all, hardly more precise or homogeneous, covering as it does the poor peasant-cum-sharecropper or labourer of Eastern India as well as the substantial *patidar* of Kheda or Bardoli with his two-storeyed house and command over Baraiya or Dubla labour.[4] 'Middle class' is equally vague and even more controversial, particularly in colonial India where subjective 'bourgeois' aspirations were so often associated with links with professions and tenurial landholding rather than industry or trade; I am using 'middle class' to stand for the groups which began asserting some kind of regional or national leadership from the 1870s onwards and which had a significantly different social composition and outlook from the princes, chiefs or zamindars who had led earlier outbursts against British rule down to and including 1857. The objectives of these leading groups could be quite diverse: national emancipation, regional self-assertion, caste or communal gains, and formulating class demands of toilers. The dialectic of leaders and led, spontaneity and discipline, was, however, not necessarily so very different.

Constructing a provisional typology of popular movements through a comparative study of regional and temporal variations may be useful for bringing out certain complexities and unsolved problems which the new historiographical trend has to tackle if it is to develop further: The intention here, as throughout the paper, is to raise questions rather than suggest definitive answers, which I certainly do not have in many cases.

There has been a tendency in our country for 'history-from-below' to get obsessed by a kind of spontaneity-consciousness debate, with two opposing stereotypes: one emphasizing the key and overriding role of nationalist ideology and leadership in allegedly giving form to sporadic discontent,[5] the other at times perhaps overstressing or romanticizing peasant spontaneity, initiative and rebelliousness through a theory of a fundamentally distinct 'peasant nationalism'. The debate has been probably more fruitful than the faction versus ideology controversy provoked by the Cambridge school some years ago. That it instils extremely restrictive, and leaves unanswered and even unasked a whole range of questions, would be clear to any reader of, say , Charles Tilly's study of the Vendee or T.W. Margadant's work on peasant resistance to Louis Napoleon's *coup de etat* of 1851.[6] I have in mind problems like the precise location of popular militancy—why certain districts or *taluks* show so much more grassroots initiative than other neighbouring areas. Gyan Pandey's beautifully worked-out explanation in terms of variations in Congress organizational strength and discipline is a major advance, but the question remains as to why the Congress controls happened to become more effective, say, in Agra or eventually Rae Bareli but not in Bara Banki during 1930-31.[7] One may also raise more general problems like possible alternative explanations of mass actions in terms of immiserization, growing strength and self-confidence of certain groups, or setback after a period of relative prosperity,[8] while it is impossible to avoid the thorny but necessary question of precise social class and/ or caste composition and of the categories of classification which would be most relevant in this connection. Another vital dimension would be possible differences in deep-rooted political and cultural traditions, for it is important to try to relate the short-term explosions with underlying long-term, trends: the 'event' with the 'conjuncture' and 'structure'.[9] And in tackling all these and many other problems, the essential tool of analysis has to be the study of variations over space and time, the comparative method expounded so eloquently by Marc Bloch.'[10]

Above all, 'history from below' has to face the problem of the ultimate relative *failure* of mass initiative in colonial India, if the justly abandoned stereotype of the eternally passive Indian peasant is not to be replaced by an opposite romantic stereotype of perennial rural rebelliousness. For an essential fact surely is that the 'subaltern' classes have remained subaltern, often surprisingly dormant despite abject misery and ample provocation, and subordinate in the end to their social 'betters' even when they do become politically active. An explanation in terms of repeated 'betrayals' by the propertied leadership, particularly Gandhi, put forward in a crude form by R.P. Dutt a generation ago and tacitly implied by many later scholars, is surely anything but satisfactory here. It implies a kind of elitism in reverse, the evil 'Jonah of Indian Revolution' successfully torpedoing mass movements, and fails to explain why the betrayer always retained so much more mass popularity than his radical critics. We have to search rather for the weaknesses internal to popular movements, and a central theme of my third section is that both the strength and the limitations of Gandhian movements transcend, the greatness or inadequacies of Gandhi as a person or of his ideology. A related problem is what may be described as the frequent interpenetration of diverse and even contradictory forms of consciousness, class, national, regional, caste or communal. A district like Shahabad in Bihar, to take one example out of many, was very active in 1857 under Kunwar Singh, plunged into bitter Hindu-Muslim riots in 1917, became a stronghold of the Kisan Sabha in the late 1930s, played a significant part in the 1942 upsurge, and was torn by communal strife again in 1946. Historians often like to demarcate between rival 'trends' of sentiment, thought and action, attributing validity to some and a lower status of 'false consciousness' to others, but the unpleasant fact remains that the separation was obviously very far from clear to contemporaries. We have to try to grasp the complex and varying interrelations between diverse elements in a hybrid 'collective mentality' of a group, class, or region.

Such limitations led up to the central fact of 1947: an achievement of political freedom successfully divorced by urban and rural propertied groups from fundamental socio-economic transformation. In the concluding section I have raised the problem of categorization of this complex and contradictory transition, and I have suggested the possible relevance here of Gramsci's concept of 'passive revolution'.

NOTES

1. The first volume of a series under that title was published just after I had completed the original draft of this paper. Ranajit Guha (ed.), *Subaltern Studies 1: Writings on South Asian History and Society* (Delhi, 1982).
2. "I am seeking to rescue the poor stockinger, the Luddite cropper, the 'obsolete' handloom weaver, the 'utopian' artisan ... from the enormous condescension of posterity". E.P. Thompson, *The Making of the English Working Class* (London, 1963), p. 12.
3. The data made available through books, research articles, and unpublished' dissertations or work-in-progress is already surprisingly massive, as I have had the occasion to discover for myself while preparing a general study of the 1885-1947 period. These include the work of David Hardiman and Ghanshyam Shah on Gujarat; Ravinder Kumar,

Neil Charlesworth and Gail Omvedt on Maharashtra; Gyan Pandey, Majid Siddiqi, and Kapil Kumar on United Provinces; Walter Hauser, K. Suresh Singh, Jacques Pouchepadass, Stephen Henningham, Saradindu Mukherji, and Alok Sheel on Bihar (unfortunately I have not seen Arvind Das's Ph.D. thesis on the same region), Benoy Chowdhuri, Kalyan Sengupta, Hitesh Sanyal, Partha Chatterjee, Sunil Sen, Tanika Sarkar and Rafiuddin Ahmed on Bengal; Amalendu Guha on Assam; Biswamoy Pati on Orissa; David Arnold on South India; Robin Jeffrey on Travancore; and D.H. Dhanagare, Stephen Dale and Conrad Wood on Malabar.

4. David Hardiman, *Peasant Nationalists of Gujarat* (Delhi, 1981), pp. 262-63.
5. For a particularly bold statement of this viewpoint, see Bipan Chandra, "Peasantry and National Integration in Contemporary India". "Nationalism helped arouse the peasant and awaken him to his own needs... Nationalism helped the peasant movement to 'stand on its feet' ...overcoming the utterly disjointed and local character of the peasant movements of the nineteenth century...". This essay is included in Bipan Chandra, *Nationalism and Colonialism in Modern India* (New Delhi, 1979), p. 345.
6. Charles Tilly, *The Vendee* (London, 1964); W. Margadant, *French Peasants in Revolt: The Insurrection of 1851* (Princeton, 1979).
7. Gyan Pandey, *Ascendancy of the Congress in Uttar Pradesh 1926-34: A Study in Imperfect Mobilization* (Delhi, 1978), Chapters 6, 7.
8. Margadant, *French Peasants,* pp. 48-50, 79, formulates this three-fold typology of economic explanations of revolt, tracing the second back to Tocqueville and the first (much more dubiously) to Marx.
9. After a period of almost total concentration on the *longue duree* inspired by Braudel, some of the *Annales* historians are now emphasizing more the need to study such interrelations.

See, for example, E. Le Roy Ladurie, "The 'Event' and the 'Long Term' in Social History: The Case of the Chouan Uprising" (1972) reprinted in his *The Territory of the Historian* (Harvester Press, 1979), as well as his fascinating *Carnival: A People's Rising in Romans* (London, 1980).

10. Mare Bloch, "A Contribution towards a Comparative History *of* European Societies" (1928). Reprinted in Bloch, *Land and Work in Medieval Europe* (London, 1967).

2

C. 1870-1917

In constructing a typology of popular movements under colonialism, it is convenient to start with a distinction between 'primary' and 'secondary' forms of resistance. This distinction was first made in the field of African studies but is being applied now increasingly also to nineteenth century India.[1] 'Primary' resistance refers to the opposition of pre-colonial, as yet largely unchanged, socio-political structures to foreign intrusion, headed by traditional elements (princes, tribal chiefs, zamindars, established religious leaders, etc.) and having in the main a 'restorative' aim.[2] 'Secondary' resistance develops somewhat later, with deeper colonial penetration; it is characterized by new types of leadership and aims going beyond simple restoration of the past (in content, if not always in form).

Primary resistance need not take much of our time here, for by the 1870s this was clearly fast declining. Its predominance up to and including 1857 is equally obvious. Relatively few historians have followed up the pioneering work of S.B. Chaudhuri twenty-five years ago on 'civil disturbances',[3] and so the role of popular initiative in such movements remains largely unexplored. A recent detailed study of popular resistance in Awadh in 1857-58 highlights the initial impetus coming from sepoys (i.e., peasants in uniform), the relatively late entry of *talukdars* when British rule had already collapsed, the big difference in numbers between regular *talukdari* retainers and the levies which fought a guerrilla war so doggedly under their leadership, and the fact that swords far exceeded firearms in the arms seizures made by the British but the fundamental features emphasized throughout remain religio-political 'restorative' aims and *talukdari* leadership (even what is, not too happily, styled '*talukdar*-peasant symbiosis').[4]

The decline in this type of resistance after 1857 was obviously connected with the major shift in British policy towards conciliation of princes and landed elements, typified by the abandonment of the doctrine of lapse and in the Awadh policy of 'sympathy' towards *talukdars.* In addition, traditional patterns of paternalism and deference were being eroded with the spread of the harsher logic of commercialization. As the 'lords of the land' became transformed into mere 'landlords' in a process analyzed recently by Metcalf,[5] Awadh peasants who had loyally followed the *talukdars* in 1857 began, already from the 1880s, to consider them their principal oppressors.[6] A third factor, deserving much greater attention than usually accorded to it, was the decline of the share of state revenue in the surplus from agriculture, benefiting zamindars as well as the upper stratum of *raiyats* (who consequently often in practice became small landlords) in ryotwari areas, and sharpening the contradictions between such groups and subordinate rural elements. From at least Mughal times down to the mid-nineteenth century, the state had been the principal appropriator of the surplus from the countryside, with groups generically described as zamindars playing a significiant but essentially subordinate role. Peasant resistance had consequently been directed in the main, against state officials, and normally led by local zamindar elements with whom the upper stratum of the *raiyats* were often associated by paternalist traditions and often by clan or caste linkages.[7] Rural rebellion in both Mughal and early colonial India consequently seems to have resembled the movements against tax-officials of the absolutist state in seventeenth century France, rather than late-medieval *jacqueries*, the Peasant War of 1525, or the anti-seigneurial explosion of 1789.[8] Post-1857 moves to extend the Permanent Settlement (which had allegedly kept Bengal loyal) proved abortive, and periodic revenue reassessments led to occasional peasant unrest and to nationalist criticism till the 1920s, but land revenue still steadily fell behind agricultural prices. The share of land revenue in gross Government of India, tax receipts fell from 43 per cent in 1880 to 23 per cent in 1920, while in Madras Presidency between 1860 and 1920, average assessment per acre of cultivated land went up from Rs. 1.7 to Rs. 2.1 during a period in which grain prices rose by between 120 and 180 per cent.[9] After the shock of the successful Bardoli *satyagraha* of 1928, efforts to hike up land revenue virtually ceased, setting a pattern which post-1947 regimes have been unwilling or unable to reverse.

Turning to forms of popular resistance not led by traditional upperclass elements, a further subdivision by the criteria of social composition and objective seems helpful. I would like to distinguish fairly sharply, first, between movements of tribals and low caste agricultural labourers or poor peasants, often very militant and occasionally far-reaching in aims, and those of relatively substantial upper and intermediate caste landholding peasants which tended to be both more limited in objectives and more pacific in methods. Within both social categories, a further sub-division has to be made, demarcating fairly direct movements of resistance to exploitation by *dikus*, moneylenders, zamindars, planters; or colonial revenue, forest or police officials from more complex and ambiguous forms in which the persistance or strengthening of traditional patterns of loyalty cut across or blurred class differences and led to caste movements and communal tensions.

My first distinction requires some further discussion, since it will play a crucial role in the subsequent analysis, and since this is yet another cardinal feature of both pre-colonial and colonial rural society which I feel has been often not given its proper importance. The myth of the relatively undifferentiated and harmonious 'village community' persisted in both nationalist and Marxist circles much longer than warranted by the data. Both R.P. Dutt and S.J. Patel, for example, assumed landless agricultural labour to have been a marginal phenomenon in pre-colonial India; and attributed its obvious later importance to processes associated with colonialism: peasant differentiation through commercialization of agriculture and over-pressure on land as rural handicrafts were ruined while population increased.[10] It is very clear now, however, that there did exist a fairly large class of often semi-servile agricultural labour even in the pre-colonial situation of a general land surplus, and that this was fundamentally connected with caste restrictions inhibiting some from working with their hands and others from becoming landholders.[11] Irfan Habib in a recent article has drawn pointed attention to the way in which this feature set apart the medieval Indian peasantry from its counterpart in Europe or China, making many petty cultivators, exploited by *jagirdars* and zamindars, themselves also exploiters of low caste or tribal labour.[12] 'Cyclical' or 'multidirectional' mobility within the peasantry, which one could have possibly expected in a land-surplus situation from the Chayanov model,[13] were thus short-circuited even before the more recent over-pressure on land, with consequences inhibiting severely the unity of the rural poor. This was a fundamental feature of the agrarian scene whose political significance I intend to explore later.

The work of historians like Hobsbawm, Rude and Thompson have made us familiar with various forms of pre-industrial popular resistance in Europe—certain types of crime, conflicts over forest laws, social banditry, millenarianism, food riots seeking to impose a just price'[14] —and it would be interesting to consider how far such categories are applicable to movements of the lowest stratum of rural society in colonial India.

The social history of crime in India is still in its infancy, but David Arnold has recently analyzed Madras police administrative reports to bring out marked correlations between years of scarcity or famine and the incidence of food riots and dacoity, as well as certain seasonal variations (the lean months from February to June being the main 'dacoity season', also September onwards if the monsoon failed). There were serious food riots in the famine year 1876 in many districts of Madras,[15] while a particularly intense wave was that of the years immediately after the First World War: 115 grain shops looted in Bombay city in early 1918, food riots in the Krishna-Godavari delta in May and in Madras city in September of the same year, and 38 *hat* looting cases with 859 convictions reported from 7 districts of Bengal in 1919-20.[16] While these are some scattered references to crowds enforcing lower prices and not simply looting markets,[17] such instances of *taxation populaire* seem to have been less common here than in eighteenth century England or France, possibly because of the absence of any firm tradition of fixation of prices by local or state authorities.[18]

Arnold has rightly criticized Hobsbawm's over-facile acceptance of the colonial theory of self-contained 'criminal tribes and castes' as representing the Indian variant of social banditry.[19] How artificial such administrative categories could become is indicated by the fact that in Kheda district of Gujarat the Baraiya and the Patanvadiya castes, comprising no less than 37 per cent of the population, were branded as 'criminal' in 1911.[20] But certain communities rendered marginal by socio-economic or political developments could turn to professional dacoity more or less as a group, while food-gathering by primitive tribes could easily become 'criminal' in the eyes of immigrant peasant settlers or administrators of forests newly 'reserved' by the state.[21] Traditions of banditry have in fact been remarkably strong in many parts of India right down to the present day. Dispossessed or otherwise down-and-out peasants and labourers would normally provide the main source of recruits for dacoit bands, though the outlaw leader could at times be a zamindar fallen on evil days, and illicit connections with local police or state officials have been and remain by no means uncommon. The typical peasant attitude to banditry is likely to be a varying compound of fear, admiration, and vicarious satisfaction in so far as the victims would normally be the better-off sections of the community. Crooke's account of Northern Indian peasant religion and folklore refers to numerous cases of deification by "criminal and nomadic tribes of notorious robbers'—like Madhukar Shah of Sagar in Central Provinces, the UP Banjara cults of the thief Mana and the freebooter Mitthu Bhukiya, or the Bihar Dom reverence for the thief Gandeh.[22] Two folk tales from Gujarat vividly reflect the complexities of the peasant-bandit relationship: The peasant named Lakha and his daughter are hailed in one story for heroically resisting the demands of Apa Devat, a notorious robber chief. But there is also the tale of Bhimo Jat and his three brothers who are forced to become outlaws after their land is seized by officers of the Thakur Sahib of Gondal for sheltering dacoits. "We give shelter to the dacoits and robbers, because otherwise they terrorize us and kidnap our children. You do not give us any protection. What else can we do?" Bhimo Jat, we are told, "plundered villagers for food. But he never harmed anyone, nor did he hold prisoners to ransom". He died heroically fighting a whole army, and he "is still thought of with pride by the people of his village".[23]Such legends resemble very closely the history of more recent real life dacoits of the same region, like Aliya the Muslim peasant of Borsad in Kheda, who lost his land through mortgage to a Brahman lawyer, committed 35 murders and 55 dacoities between 1918 and 1923, had occasional links with a rich *patidar* headman who received his stolen goods and also at times with some policemen, but who still retained a social bandit-type reputation within his own community. Aliya was hanged in 1924, but "even today the Muslims of Borsad town worship at the grave of Aliya Pir".[24]

Social banditry of this type was an endemic feature of many pre-industrial societies, varying with the extent of economic distress but providing a kind of historical constant in a more long-term sense—"a protest,... [but] a modest and unrevolutionary protest",[25] at best righting some individual wrongs, but not aiming at or connected with any structural change. Late colonial India, however, also saw numerous 'transformative' rebellions, particularly in tribal areas. Too much should not be made of this distinction between tribals and other sections of the rural poor, for apart from some isolated and really primitive food-gatherers, the *adivasis* were and are very much a part of Indian society as the lowest stratum of peasants subsisting through shifting cultivation, agricultural labourers, and, increasingly, 'coolies' recruited for work in distant plantations, mines and factories. But the characteristic tribal terrain with its hills and forests and undeveloped communications is obviously more suited to guerrilla resistance than more settled parts of the countryside. Tribal social organisation, while seldom entirely undifferentiated and often considerably influenced by shifts towards a caste pattern (the 'tribe-caste continuum'), still tends to retain a kind of unity lost in the fragmented structure of fully-developed caste Hindu society.

Tribal movements in the post-1857 phase tended to acquire two new features: a growing emphasis on the issue of forest rights, and a shift in the initiative for rebellion from traditional chiefs to prophets, who emphasized the need for internal socio-religious change to 'revitalize' the community and at times promised sudden, miraculous change of a 'millenarian' type.[26] Colonial rule and its accompanying commercialization affected tribal societies adversely in a variety of ways. It strengthened already present tendencies towards penetration of tribal areas by outsiders from the plains (moneylenders, traders, landgrabbers, labour contractors, etc.), enforced novel conceptions of absolute private property and alienation through sale for indebtedness on groups with fairly strong traditions of communal landholding (like the *khuntkatti* tenure in Chota Nagpur, for instance), ruthlessly exploited tribals as a reserve of cheap 'coolie' labour via, the indenture system, and—more ambiguously—offered through missionary activity some education and possibility of social ascent combined with a wholesale assault on established cultural patterns. But the progressive tightening from the 1870s and 80s of colonial state control over forest areas for purposes of revenue and conservation provided perhaps the most deeply-felt grievance of all. The ban on shifting cultivation (*jhum* in Eastern India, *podu* in Andhra) was particularly disastrous for tribals and poor peasants in forest areas, for unlike settled plough-cultivation it did not require cattle or manure.[27] For millennia (and by no means in India alone)[28] the virgin forest had provided a variety of 'free goods' for the rural poor—timber for fuel, dwellings and tools, grazing facilities, edible roots and plants, fish and game—and Kosambi has emphasized the prodigality of sub-tropical nature as a possible explanation of the remarkable survival in our country of primitive food-gathering side by side with settled agriculture and urban civilization.[29] Nor was the alienation one of a purely economic or material kind. The sudden clamping down of restrictions on the use of or even entry into 'reserved' forests rudely disrupted deep-rooted and profoundly evocative cultural patterns.[30]

Such pressures, combined with a loss of faith in traditional chiefs due to the failure of the first wave of 'primary resistance', led to 'revitalization' movements of internal religious and socio-cultural reform under messiahs who at times borrowed elements from Christianity or Hinduism. The millenarian pattern typically included brief spells of exaltation and rebellion in the hope of immediately turning the world upside down, followed by periods of quiescence when the movement turned into an inward-looking sect, deferring the prospect of miraculous change to a distant future or the after-life.[31] The brief period of revolutionary hope was often associated also with rumours about the imminent, collapse of British rule—an association by no means confined, as we shall see, to such 'primitive' rebellions alone.

Among the Santals, the Kharwar or Sapha Hor movement developed in the 1870s after the failure of the great 1855 rebellion. It concentrated in the main on preaching monotheism and internal social reform, but was turning towards agrarian issues before the arrest of its first leader Bhaggirath.[32] The Ulgulan (Great Tumult) of Birsa Munda (1899-1900) in the Ranchi region is too well-known (through the study by K. Suresh Singh) to require much discussion here. We may note, however, that Birsa emerged in the wake of the failure of the *sardari larai* of the early 90s led by tribal chiefs against the erosion of *khuntkatti* joint tenures (and after missionaries had also failed to provide redress). This son of a poor sharecropper of Chalked, having undergone some Christian and then Vaishnava influence and participated in a struggle to defend village waste lands against forest laws in 1893-94, claimed from 1895 onwards to be a prophet of a supreme monotheistic God, with miraculous healing powers as well as the power to turn guns and bullets to water.[33] Fiery night meetings in the forest against "Thikadars and Jagirdars and Rajas and Hakims and Christians" led up to attacks on churches and police stations in December 1899-January 1900. These attacks were sufficiently widespread to cause a real panic in Ranchi and some concessions on the *khuntkatti* issue a few years later. Though Birsa was quickly captured and died in jail in June 1900, a Birsa sect has survived among the Mundas. This sect preaches monotheism and puritanical social reform in the expectation of a distant deliverance, but not immediate revolt to achieve a new world.[34] The Tana Bhagat movement among the neighbouring Oraons also reveals this characteristic oscillation: beginning in 1914 as a sect calling for monotheism, abstention from meat, liquor and tribal dances, and a return to shifting cultivation, it briefly took on a more radical millenarian colour next year as rumours spread of the coming of a saviour variously identified with Birsa or a 'German' or 'Kaiser Baba', but lapsed back into relative quietism following repression and the end of the World War.[35]

The forests and hills of south Rajasthan and northwest Gujarat were another centre of tribal unrest. In 1868, the Naikda tribe of Panch Mahal (Gujarat), attacked police stations in a bid to establish a *dharmaraj*. Here religious messianism seems to have merged with memories of the recent Rebellion, for an 1857 survivor, Rupsingh Gobar, led the attacks along with the messianic leader Joria.[36] Some forty years later, a Hinduizing temperance and purification movement led by Govind Guru among the Bhils of Banswara, Sunth and Dungarpur states (adjoining Mewar) and of Panch Mahal district in Gujarat suddenly flared up into a brief attempt to set up an independent Bhil raj in November 1913. Four thousand Bhils assembled on Mangad hill, and the British were able to disperse them only after considerable resistance in what seems to have been a kind of semi-symbolic battle; rather reminiscent of the last-ditch stand of the Birsaites on Sail Rakab hill a few years ago.[37]

At the other end of the country, the Kacha Nagas of Cachar district of Assam had attacked the whites in 1882, inspired by a messianic belief in a sixteenth-century Bhim Raja who was said to be sleeping in a cave, and more immediately by a miracle-worker named Shambhudan, who claimed that his magic made his followers immune from bullets.[38] The millenarian note was absent, however, from the major revolt of the Thadoe Kukis in Manipur in 1917-1919 which was led by powerful established chiefs and did not extend to the Kabui or 'old' Kukis who had a more democratic kind of tribal organization. British efforts to recruit tribal labour for menial service on the Western Front provided the immediate issue, but there were also other grievances like *pothang* (forced labour to carry baggages of officials or to build roads), a heavy house tax despite near-famine conditions, and British efforts to stop *jhum*. Further complexities were produced by intra-tribal feuds (Thadoe vs. Kabui) and a dynastic rivalry (with rebels developing some connections with a claimant to the Manipur throne). These features have been pointed out by Gautam Bhadra in an analysis refreshingly free from the usual simplistic treatment of tribal movements as homogeneous entities. Guerrilla war went on for two years, affecting a population of 40,000 in an area of 6000 square miles.[39]

But the principal area of virtually endemic tribal rebellion lay in the forests and hills lying to the north of the Godavari, constituting under the British the Godavari and Vizagapatam Agency Tracts, extending northwards into Bastar, Malkangiri and Koraput, and inhabited by Koyas, Konda Doras and Kondhs largely dependent on shifting cultivation (*podu*). The epicentre was Chodavaram, the 'Rampas' country (so-called by the British after the family name of its traditional chief or *mansabdar*) along with the neighbouring Gudem region.[39a] The earlier revolts (1840, 1845, 1858, 1861, 1862) were led by subordinate hill-chiefs (*muttadars*) against their *mansabdar* superior, with whom the British had come to an arrangement in 1813, and who had utilized British protection to extort "a considerable revenue from taxes on fuel and grazing and other unauthorized cesses".[40] The biggest rising of all—that of 1879-80, which affected 5000 square miles—had its epicentre in Chodavaram and Rekapalle in Godavari, and extensions towards the Golkonda Hills of Vizagapatam, parts of Malkangiri, and Bastar.[41] The rising is sufficiently well-documented to allow a more concrete analysis of the pattern of tribal grievances and resistance. In Chodavaram, oppression by the *mansabdar* (now taking the form of eviction of old *muttadars*, as well as the *kalapapannu* and *poolary* taxes on wood-cutting and grazing) remained a principal grievance, though the Madras official Sullivan noted a general impression that the British were fully behind the *mansabdar* and so had the ultimate responsibility for tribal woes.[42] The immediate cause of the rising, however, was the recent extension of Madras *abkari* laws to the Rampa area, with the auction-purchaser of the toddy *ijara* imposing a heavy *chigurupannu* tax (to which the *mansabdar* promptly added *modalupannu* cess) on what had been not only an age-old free good ("It is never collected since creation", complained a captured rebel)[43] but "an absolute necessity of life to the hill-tribes during certain months of the year".[44] In neighbouring Rekapalle (transferred along with Bhadrachalam from CP to Madras in 1875), the attempt to impose forest laws, which had not yet been enforced in Chodavaram, became the major issue. Once again an ancient tradition was being rudely violated through restrictions on *podu* which Sullivan considered "wholly unnecessary".[45] Tribals in both districts also complained about increasing penetration by Komati trader-moneylenders from the plains.[46] Petty exactions by local police officials was another major grievance.[47] The revolt which began in March 1879 with attacks on police stations developed into a guerrilla war which the British could suppress only in November 1880 after deploying six regiments of infantry, two companies of sappars and miners, and some cavalry.[48] The rebels, noted an official report, had only a few matchlocks and muskets, but were accompanied by "a large rabble with sticks, bows and arrows", and owed their success to "the large extent of dense jungles, and... the thorough sympathy of the people..."[49] There are no references to any millenarian dimension in this rising, possibly because (as with the Thadoe Kukis) the leadership came mainly from established *muttadars*.

The British responded to this formidable rising by relaxing *abkari* regulations, pensioning off the *mansabdar*, instituting direct revenue arrangements with the *muttadars*, and (from 1892) buying the support of *muttadars* for forest law enforcement by giving them extra allowances.[50] Far from ending unrest all this seems to have imparted an even clearer anti-British edge to tribal discontent by removing the *mansabdar* buffer. The conversion of *muttadars* into collaborators opened the way for a new type of leadership with religious and millenarian overtones. A rising in 1886 was led by Surla Ramanna and Rajana Anantayya, a young tribal and an ex-constable and teacher who claimed to be incarnations of Rama and Hanuman and called their rebel band *Rama Dandu* (Rama's army). Anantayya also made an interesting 'proto-nationalist' appeal to the Maharaja of Jeypore (in Koraput), revealing some awareness of broader political developments:

> Is it good, if the English be in our country? .... We ...should wage war with the English. The Russians are also troubling the English. If the assistance of men and arms are supplied to me, I will play Rama's part.[51]

In 1900 in Vizagapatam Agency, a Konda Dow named Korra Mallaya

> pretended that he was inspired ...gathered round him a camp of 4-5000 people from various parts of the agency ...gave out that he was a reincarnation of one of the five Pandava brothers [and] that his infant son was the god Krishna; that he would drive out the English and rule the country himself; and that, to effect this, he would arm his followers with bamboos, which should be turned by magic into guns, and would change the weapons of the authorities into water.

The rebels drilled with bamboos "rudely fashioned to resemble guns"; they were shot down by a police party on 7 May, with 11 killed. The Konda Doras of Vizag, incidentally, were worshippers of the Pandava brothers.[52]

Tightening of state control over forests (annual forest revenues in Godavari district went up from Rs. 21,000 in the 1870s to over Rs. 2 lakhs by 1904-05)[53] remained a perennial source of discontent in all tribal areas. The very primitive food-gathering Chenchus of the Nallamalai hills (Cuddapah and Nellore districts of present-day south Andhra), for instance, found their traditional rights to forest products being increasingly restricted by the government from 1898 onwards, though the latter were somewhat inhibited by the fear that pure repression could lead to the total destruction by fire of the Nallamalai forests.[54] In predominantly tribal princely states, even disputed successions often developed connections with forest grievances, and quickly took on a strongly anti-British colour. The rising in Bastar in 1910 was led by a former *diwan* who was claiming the throne, but the main cause was again the recent imposition of forest regulations banning shifting cultivation and free use of forest produce. The rebels disrupted communications, attacked police stations and forest outposts, burnt schools (which were being built by forced labour and compulsory levies on tribals), and even tried to besiege Jagdalpur town.[55] In the Orissa feudatory state of Daspalia in October 1914, a Khond rebellion over a succession dispute quickly took on a different colour, as rumours spread that a war had started and soon "there would be no Sahabs left in the country" and the Khonds would "live under their own rule". The British feared a general Khond rising which could "set ablaze the whole of the vast inaccessible mountain tracts stretching along the Eastern Ghats so far as Kalahandi and Bastar.", and so went about burning Khond villages.[56] During the war years, there was yet another *fituri* (rising) in the Rampa area in 1916, while, as among the Thadoe Kukis, recruitment of tribal labour for the war effort led to a revolt in Mayurbhanj.

Movements of settled peasant communities in colonial India usually had more limited objectives and employed much less violent methods than tribal revolts—with one major exception: the Mappilas of Malabar, with their 32 recorded outbreaks between 1836 and 1919, culminating in the very major rebellion of 1921. The agrarian dimensions of Mappila unrest have been repeatedly emphasised ever since Logan in 1881 drew pointed attention to the ways in which British rule with its usual insistence on absolute proprietary rights had reestablished and vastly enhanced the position of Namboodri and Nayar *jenmis* (many of whom had been driven out by Tipu Sultan) and correspondingly worsened the conditions of the largely Muslim leaseholders and cultivators. Sixty-two out of the 82 victims of Mappila attacks between 1836 and 1919 were upper-caste Hindus (22 Namboodris and 34 Nayars), about 58 of them were either *jenmis* or moneylenders (or both),[57] and links with, *jenmi*- tenant disputes are clear in 12 out of the 32 incidents.[58] The vast majority of the activists were petty tenants or agricultural labourers,[59] but they clearly enjoyed the sympathy of the entire Mappila community, being revered as *shahids* in a holy war. The agrarian grievances were hardly unique to the Mappilas; what makes these 'outrages' so remarkable were their highly localised nature and extremely distinctive form. The incidents were largely confined to two *talukas* of south Malabar (Ernad and Walavanad). The actual participants were relatively few (only 351 in all 32 cases). After murdering their chosen upper-caste Hindu targets, the assailants invariably attempted a kind of collective suicide instead of trying to abscond, frontally confronting the police and fighting till the end to achieve the status of *shahid* (no less than 319 out of 351 died fighting). Conrad Wood relates these peculiarities to the settlement pattern of Ernad and Walavanad (as distinct from north Malabar or the coastal area): scattered homesteads with very poor communications instead of nuclear villages, making collective mass resistance difficult, and leading to a situation in which the mosque was the one unifying social centre.[60] One might hazard a parallel here with the Mauges region of western France, the heart of the Vendee counter-revolution in 1793 with its dispersed settlements and priestly domination as contrasted to neighbouring Val Saumurois with agglomerated villages, greater urban-rural integration, and republican sympathies.[61]

The recent study by Stephen Dale, however, emphasises religious and cultural traditions rather than agrarian grievances alone, with some justice, perhaps, for there was no lack of oppressed Hindu peasants in Malabar, rack-rented and evicted by *jenmis*, whose protest at times took the form of banditry, but never the distinctive suicidal terrorism adopted by the Mappilas.[62] Dale tries to trace the roots of Mappila militancy back to the bitter hostility to the infidel whites generated already in the sixteenth century by Portuguese seizure of the spice trade and forcible conversions—a spirit reflected in Zaynal-Din's *Tuhfat-al-Mujahidin* of the 1580s or in ballads honouring *Shahids* in the anti-Portuguese struggle like *Kotturpalli Mala* (still popular today). There were even a few cases of suicidal attacks on Europeans and Nayar landlords already in the early eighteenth century, anticipating the characteristic pattern of the 'outrages' of the nineteenth century.[63] The number of mosques in Malabar went up from 637 in 1831 to 1058 by 1851;[64] and there were large scale conversions to Islam by untouchable Cherumars for whom this meant a definite rise in social status.[65] The major ideological stimulus for Mappila outbreaks in the 1840s and early 50s came from the Tannal of Mambram mosque near Tirurangadi, Sayyid Fadl (exiled by the British in 1852), who preached that it was lawful to murder a Hindu *jenmi* evicting a Muslim tenant, and that the honorific plural should not be used when addressing Nayars.[66] Mappila war songs contained vivid descriptions of the often frankly carnal pleasures of paradise awaiting *shahids*.[67] The appeal of the Islamic conception of paradise to people deprived of most earthly pleasures by poverty should not be underestimated. This is indicated by the curious fact that a translation of the Koran seems to have been one source for the amazingly radical ideas of Menocchio, the sixteenth century Italian miller recently resurrected from Inquisition records by Carlo Ginzburg's fascinating study.[68]

Mappila rural terrorism, which probably did impose some checks on *jenmi* oppression, thus represented a kind of defensive millenarianism, promising heavenly pleasures to *shahids* and vengeance for specific acts of injustice, not a wholesale this-worldly transformation. But there is at least one reference to millenarianism of a more positive kind. The *Hal Illakkam* sect (literally, "frenzy-raising") in Ernad in 1843 was preaching "that a ship would arrive with the necessary arms, provisions and money for 40,000 men" to liberate the country—an exact echo, strangely enough, of the Pacific 'cargo-cults' analysed by Peter Worsley.[69] And in 1927 rumours that British rule was collapsing before the Non-Cooperation—Khilafat onslaught set off a wholesale mass rebellion among the Mappilas of Malabar.

Food riots, social banditry, or millenarian rebellions remained very distant things for the new intelligentsia which by the late nineteenth century was emerging as the bearer of both patriotic ideology and of various types of more 'sectional' awareness emphasizing communal, caste or regional affinities. Nationalist journals like the *Bengalee* wrote one or two articles sympathizing with Birsa Munda[70]—after his revolt had been safely crushed—and the Congress in the 1890s passed a number of resolutions critical of the forest laws.[71] But the prevalent attitude ranged from indifference to hostility, and there is at least one recorded instance in which food rioters sacked a Congress leader's house, no doubt because he was also a landlord and moneylender.[72] The solitary exception is the strange case of Vasudeo Balwant Phadke in 1879; a Chitpavan clerk who dreamt of reestablishing a Hindu raj by forming a secret band financed through dacoities, but whose anticipation of revolutionary terrorism differed sharply from the later pattern in its recruitment of lowcaste Ramoshis and Dhangars. The outcome was a kind of social banditry, which seems to have persisted for some years in this part of Maharashtra, even after Phadke himself had been captured.[73]

Turning from tribals and Mappilas to movements like the Pabna disturbances or the Deccan riots of the 1870s, we enter a rather different world. The issues were not too dissimilar: defence or assertion of tenant rights against zamindari rent-extortion, *abwabs,* and eviction mainly in Permanent Settlement areas; moneylender oppression or revenue and canal water rate enhancements in raiyatwari regions; and exploitation by white indigo planters. But the initiative and the bulk of the support for these movements came from relatively better off sections of the peasantry. Thus Pabna was a district with a lot of double-cropping and a flourishing trade in jute, where more than 50 per cent of the cultivators had managed to win occupancy rights, and the movement there never touched on the grievances of subordinate *korfa raiyats* or the large seasonal immigrant force of agricultural labourers.[74] The Maharashtra Deccan had witnessed some rich peasant development during the cotton boom of the 1860s. As in Pabna, unrest was sparked off by attempts to reverse a trend towards relative prosperity, through zamindar counter-offensive in the one case and moneylender exploitation in the other. In the raiyatwari areas, the *raiyats* paying revenue to the state and complaining of enhancements could at times be in reality small landlords and not actual cultivators. The movements of such groups were not necessarily always non-violent, but they had specific limited objectives, lacked millenarian dimensions, and the rumours that at times stimulated them were, significantly enough, not of the imminent collapse of British rule but of some pro-peasant measures said to have been taken by the rulers. Middle class nationalist interest in and sympathy for such limited movements was considerably more in evidence than in the case of tribal revolts, though there remained numerous hesitations and ambivalences here till the coming of Gandhi, and even later.

In the Pabna disturbances of 1873, best known among a series of movements in a number of East Bengal districts provoked by zamindar efforts to restrict the scope of occupancy rights created by Act X of 1859, peasants of Yusufshahi *pargana* fought back the claims of 'high landlordism' through largely legalistic and predominantly peaceful methods. They organized an agrarian league which raised funds to meet litigation expenses (for the 'Rampa' tribals, in contrast, the law court had been an utterly alien institution)[75] and used collective non-payment of rent as a weapon to win specific demands like an end to arbitrarily short standards of measurement (which automatically enhanced the cultivated area and therefore the rent), abolition of illegal cesses, and some reduction in rents.[76] Even the most radical demand occasionally raised by the Pabna peasants—to be "ryots of Queen of England"[77]—reveal no trace of conscious anti-imperialism; but rather an appeal to the distant overlord as against the immediate oppressor, not uncommon in peasant movements elsewhere.[78] A proclamation by Lieutenant Governor Campbell in July 1873 permitting peaceful combinations by peasants seems in fact to have been a major source of encouragement.[79] As for middle class attitudes, professional groups with less connection, with big zamindari (who were soon to form the Indian Association as the rival of the landlord-dominated British Indian Association) did show a certain sympathy for the demands of the occupancy *raiyats*, balanced however by a fear of "excesses".[80] The Indian Association even organized some *raiyat* meetings on the eve of the Tenancy Act of 1885 demanding preservation and extension of occupancy rights. But the claims of *korfa raiyats*, sharecroppers and agricultural labourers went completely by default; whether in the Pabna movement, the Indian Association agitation, or Government legislation, and no emphasis was ever placed on linking up occupancy rights with actual cultivation.[81] The ultimate effect of this entire period of agrarian unrest and tenancy legislation in Bengal was to foster the growth of *jotedar* groups, as exploitative and parasitic as the zamindars they gradually displaced.

Despite the presence among the leaders of the Pabna league of Ishan Chandra Roy and Shambhu Pal side by side with Khoodi Mollah, the bulk of the Pabna peasants happened to be Muslims while their zamindars were Hindus. Yet the efforts of the *Hindoo Patriot* to brand the movement as communal were largely unsuccessful, though a generation later the 1906-07 disturbances in Mymensingh with a considerable anti-zamindar and anti-*mahajan* content would be immediately interpreted in religious terms alone, by both Hindu and Muslim middle-class opinion.[82] One may note a parallel with the Mappila attacks on Hindu *jenmis*, with few repercussions outside Malabar throughout the nineteenth century, but which in 1921 included a novel emphasis on forcible conversions, and immediately led to all-India Hindu *Shuddhi* and *Sangathan* movements. Middle-class nationalism and communalism, as we shall see, developed 'populist' dimensions at about the same time, with consequences ultimately disastrous for the unity of the country.

The Deccan riots of May 1875, affecting 33 villages in 6 *talukas* of Ahmednagar district, were somewhat more violent than the Pabna disturbances, but hardly more radical. The sudden fall in prices[83] as the cotton boom was succeeded by a slump, accompanied by revenue enhancements in certain areas, made repayment of debts very difficult for the richer or more enterprising peasants who, banking on the high prices, had borrowed heavily from *sowcars* during the 1860s. The target of the riots was therefore the *sowcar*, but an official report noted "the absence of serious crime... [as]...a very remarkable feature in the outbreak", with the peasants interested only in seizure and destruction of debt-bonds. The villagers were often led by their headmen (*patels*), and it seems that official enquiries connected with the preparation of a gazetteer had led to rumours that "Government was enquiring into the ryots', circumstances, and that Her Majesty had ordered the *sowcars* to, give up their lands".[84] Significantly enough, only immigrant Marwari *sowcars* were attacked, and not indigenous elements who had turned to trade or moneylending (like the *khots of* Ratnagiri). In Bengal, too, the rich peasant or *jotedar*-turned moneylender was seldom attacked, unlike the Marwari or Bengali usurers among Santals or the Sahas among East Bengal Muslims.[85] A successful member of the broad community of landholding peasants, however exploitative, would be envied, admired and often looked up to for favours and leadership.[86]

The Poona nationalist press did express considerable sympathy for the Deccan *raiyats*, but significantly enough, it tended to blame excessive revenue pressure rather than moneylender exploitation as primarily responsible for peasant woes.[87] Revenue enhancement in fact was the one type of agrarian grievance which won unequivocal support from the patriotic intelligentsia, since it fitted in with the general drain of wealth scheme, basic to the emerging ideology of middle-class nationalism,[88] and had (unlike issues like zamindari or moneylender exploitation) no divisive potential setting Indians against Indians. But the great distance between the intelligentsia and the peasant world in the pre-Gandhian era kept nationalist involvement in no-revenue movements fairly minimal still, and the peasants seem to have fought back revenue hikes through indigenous methods possibly having a long history behind them. The basic forms were not insurrection—very difficult, if not impossible, for a disarmed countryside with well-developed communications, unlike tribal pockets—but petitions, collective refusals of revenue, and mass emigration, buttressed very often by appeals to caste loyalties. The leadership came from local notables or the upper stratum of the peasantry who would be the principal revenue-payers, and such movements did not disrupt the traditional structure of hierarchical subordination within the rural community.

In the Kamrup and Darrang districts of Assam, a revenue hike of 50-70 per cent in 1893 was met by *raij mels*—mass assemblies of villagers, led by the rural elite of Brahmans, Gossains and Dolois, which enforced non-payment of revenue through the weapon of social boycott or ostracism of those who broke the popular consensus. There was also some looting of bazaars, and two cases of police firing, at Rangiya and Patharaghat. Urban nationalist support was confined to resolutions of the Jorhat Sarvajanik Sabha and speeches on the floor of legislative councils.[89] The intervention of Tilak and the Poona Sarvajanik Sabha he had recently captured during the Maharashtra Deccan famine of 1896-97 was more substantial, and seriously alarmed the government. Agents were sent into the countryside to hold meetings and distribute pamphlets educating the peasant about his right to demand revenue remissions under the Famine Code in a year of scarcity, and some shortlived no-revenue combinations were started in Thana, Kolaba and Ratnagiri. The basic autonomy of the peasant movement was revealed, however, both by the looting of grain shops (which middle class nationalists of course had never advocated)[90] and the continuation of popular resistance well after the urban agitators had withdrawn and Tilak had been jailed on a different issue. Instances of distraint of movable property for non-payment of revenue in the Central Division of Bombay Presidency went up from an annual average of 26 during 1892-97 to 2269 in 1898-99.[91] In Gujarat, still a backwater so far as urban Congress nationalism was concerned, a powerful no-revenue campaign was organized during the famine of 1899-1900 when the government refused adequate remissions, with village leaders maintaining solidarity through caste boycott of those paying revenue. The *kunbi-patidar* peasants of Kheda had enjoyed a period of prosperity in the late nineteenth century from expanding markets for tobacco and dairy produce. But this was rudely disrupted by plague and famine. The peasants here also had a well- established tradition of *hijrat:* collective migration to escape excessive tax burdens, which was specifically mentioned and justified even by the basic text of the influential Swaminarayan religious sect.[92] Tilak has been occasionally hailed for anticipating Gandhi through his 1896-97 no-revenue campaign; the honour properly belongs much more to the peasantry whose traditional armoury included most of the weapons (collective non-payment, social boycott, migration) to be used under the Mahatma's leadership from the 1920s.

The second major example of a pre-Gandhian linkage between nationalism and agrarian unrest was provided by the Punjab in 1907, with the movements of Chenab canal colonists against bureaucratic control by white colonization officers, Bari Doab peasants against an increase in the canal tax, and Rawalpindi protests against a land-revenue hike. The prosperous Sikh and Muslim canal colonists (land had been given in large blocs to peasant immigrants, ex-soldiers; and urban investors; and the estates at times exceeded 2500 acres) were certainly quite capable of organizing an independent agitation.[93] Though Lajpat Rai was deported in May 1907 for allegedly inciting the peasants, his autobiography reveals him to have been rather unenthusiastic about the matter. He did address a couple of meetings of Chenab colonists at Lyallpur, but only with considerable hesitation. The more radical Ajit Singh, however, did carry on an active no-revenue campaign, and frightened Lajpat by his seditious talk.[94]

The disjunction between early nationalism and peasant unrest is revealed clearly also by the Bijolia movement in Mewar from 1905. At a time when in far-off Bengal patriotic intellectuals like R.C. Dutt, D.L. Roy, Abanindranath and Rabindranath were writing novels, plays, stories and poems hailing the chivalry and heroism of the medieval Rajputs of Mewar, the latter's modern descendants were combining servility towards the British with the grossest forms of feudal exploitation of the peasantry. In the Bijolia *jagir* of Mewar, the burden of no less than 86 different cesses imposed by the *thikanadars* led peasants in 1905 and again in 1913 to collectively refuse to cultivate lands and attempt a mass migration to neighbouring areas—the classic pattern of peasant protest through flight, so often mentioned in medieval sources.[95] The leadership at Bijolia was provided initially by a *sadhu*, Sitaram Das; but a link with nationalism was provided, more or less accidentally, by the internment in that region of an ex-revolutionary, Vijay Singh Pathik. Pathik and a disgruntled Udaipur official, Manik Lal Verma, were leading a no-tax movement in Bijolia again in 1916, and both later became prominent Congress leaders.[96]

Peasant resistance to white indigo planters forms a rather special category. The racial aspect here had aroused considerable middle-class sympathy already in the Bengal 'Blue Mutiny' of 1859-60.[97] Planters in Champaran at first had a somewhat easier time, for unlike Central Bengal this was an outlying region and a mutually profitable arrangement had been reached with the local zamindars, with Europeans becoming tenure-holding *thikadars* in the Permanent Settlement hierarchy. But there was already some resistance in 1867-68, winning a reduction on the land compulsorily put under indigo from 5-6 to 3 *kathas* per *bigha* (the *tinkathia* system). Tensions sharpened after *c* 1900 following the decline of the indigo demand in face of German synthetic dye competition. Planters sought compensation through rent enhancements *(sharahbeshi)* and lump-sum payments (*tawan*) in return for releasing peasants from the obligation to grow indigo. There was a major movement in the Motihari-Bettiah region in 1905-08, affecting 400 square miles and involving the murder of a white factory manager and 57 criminal cases.[98] The resistance over the next decade took the forms of petitions, cases and efforts to get the support of Bihar Congress leaders and journalists, and it was as a part of this ongoing confrontation that Raj Kumar Shukla contacted Gandhi at the Lucknow Congress in 1916. While many sections of rural society had their grievances about the planters,[99] the initiative for organizing what Jacques Pouchepadass has described as "upward pressure from the rural masses themselves"[100] came from the peasant upper crust which resented "the lost opportunity of doing business which the indigo obligation represented" as prices of foodgrains and sugar cane rose with a growing export trade from Champaran.[101] Raj Kumar Shukla himself had 20 bighas of land in a district with an average holding of 3½ bighas, plus, a small moneylending business. Poorer sections, both in 1905-08 and in 1917, were rallied also through religious and caste sanctions, with threats of social boycott and peasants taking oaths before village shrines, non-compliance carrying the penalties of beef for Hindus and pork for Muslims.[102]

Thus a recurrent feature of most popular movements was the reliance on traditional community consciousness and sanctions based on it, whether tribal, caste or religious. It is noteworthy that tribals uprooted from their native earth and clan, linkages apparently also lost much of their militancy. Despite atrocious, semi-servile conditions, Assam tea coolies recruited in large part from tribal areas failed to develop organized protest movements—as distinct from sporadic cases of violence—till a fairly late date. The strength of traditional ties is evident even among social groups connected with the genuinely new capitalist sector of the economy. With the exception of the Parsis, whose relative weight within the Indian bourgeoisie has declined over time, business groups in our country have been marked on the whole not by any unequivocally 'modern' ideology, but rather by the strength of institutions of joint family and caste—elements which according to some historians actually go some way towards explaining the remarkable Marwari success-story.[103] In the Surat protests against the salt duty in 1844, revised weights and measures in 1848, income tax in 1860, and a license tax in 1878, (which judging by most of the issues must have had a strong merchant component) the main weapon was the closing of shops *(hartal)* organized by caste and community leaders, and government officials were sometimes threatened with social boycott.[104] The importance of traditional forms in the early labour movement is indicated by the existence, at least in Bengali, of a purely indigenous synonym for the strike *(dharmaghat)*, unlike much of the remaining vocabulary of the working-class and socialist movement.[105] The term indicates both early and spontaneous origins (in fact, probably a carry-over from peasant no-rent movements, which were described as *dharmaghat by* the Derozian Pyarichand Mitra in 1846),[106] and a connection with some kind of religious vow. During a strike at the Kharagpur railway workshop in September 1906, the leaders are said to have brought the workers out "under the penalty, in the case of Hindus, of being made to eat cow's meat, and in the case of Muhammadans, pig's flesh".[107] Dipesh Chakrabarty has recently emphasized the importance of 'community consciousness', as distinct from a unified and clear recognition of class, among jute mill workers in and around Calcutta in the 1890s. Muslim workers demanded holidays for *Id* or *Muharram*, Hindus for *Rathajatra*, and there were occasional fratricidal riots over issues like cow slaughter.[108]

It is true that communal or caste divisions did not prevent united action against employers; and as in peasant movements, the initiative in early strikes came almost entirely from the workers themselves. Late nineteenth century middle class interest in industrial or plantation labour as embodied in the efforts of Sasipada Banerji, Dwarakanath Ganguli, or N.M. Lokhande did not go beyond philanthropy. Swadeshi barristers like A.C. Banerji and A.K. Ghosh who led strikes and helped to start unions in Bengal during 1905-08 seem to have done so usually after workers had gone on strike and sought their help.[109a] Though some organizational work in Bombay city by Extremists through jobbers did precede the great protest strike following Tilak's transportation in July 1908, the main initiative again probably came from mill-hands, for Tilak's speeches in the factory area had been remarkably free of class war tones.[109b] The Bombay strike, along with *hartals* in Calcutta on 16 October 1905, protest strikes in Rawalpindi after the deportation of Lajpat Rai, and in the Tuticorin-Tinnevelli area in February-March 1908 following the arrest of Subramaniya Siva and Chidambaram Pillai, revealed that the Indian working class was not incapable of political strikes.[109c] But the oscillation between united class action and caste or communal conflicts was never entirely overcome, even the great Girni Kamgar strike in Bombay in 1928 being followed within a few months by a communal riot.

The persistence of pre-industrial traditions is nothing peculiar to the Indian working class. Herbert Gutman, for instance, has emphasized the importance of "artisan work-habits and diverse ethnic ...subcultures" in the formation of the American industrial labour force from consecutive waves of immigrants.[110] The essential problem really lies in the specific nature of these traditions. As E.P. Thompson has shown so brilliantly, the making of the English working class was enormously helped by the rich tradition of artisan radicalism which had preserved and extended the more democratic aspects of the English bourgeois revolution of the seventeenth century. However, the Indian tribals and peasants, or dispossessed tribals, peasants and ruined artisans sucked into factories, had little to fall back upon except sectional, and often divisive, ties of kinship, region, caste or religion. Caste and religion did play an important part, as Irfan Habib has argued, in the organization of peasant revolts in Mughal India,[111] while even for the twentieth century, E.M.S. Namboodiripad once remarked that caste associations were at times "the form in which the peasant masses rose in struggle against feudalism".[111] But the extent to which caste and religious loyalties have often cut across or blurred class differences and led to disastrous internal divisions is of course very obvious.

So far as caste is concerned, I feel the crucial problem lies in the combination, in varying proportions, of two contradictory aspects in the caste-class relationship. Caste has often had a congruence with class sufficiently strong to enable the articulation of genuine socio-economic demands through the language and forms of caste. But this is combined with an asymmetry in detail which tends to blurr class lines and foster various forms of sectional or 'false' consciousness. Thus, throughout the country, landlords tended to come from the upper castes, peasant landholders to belong to what are now usually called the 'intermediate' castes, while the poorest peasants and landless labourers would comprise the lowest castes and the untouchables. But there have always been exceptions, and the system has been flexible enough to permit upward mobility through 'Sanskritization' in response to economic or other changes. One or two concrete examples might indicate the complexities. In the Rae Bareli district of the United Provinces in the early twentieth century, the bulk of the landed proprietors were Rajputs or Brahmans, but these castes also held 13 per cent and 14.5 per cent respectively of tenant land, which they usually enjoyed on specially favoured, lower rent conditions. Such terms (combined with, and often related to, kinship connections with landlords) would naturally encourage loyalties towards the zamindar patron rather than combinations with fellow-tenants of lower castes paying higher rents. Conversely, Ahirs and Kurmis were predominantly tenants, but they did hold 1000 and 15,600 acres respectively as proprietors also.[112] David Hardiman's micro-study of Kheda district in Gujarat highlights yet another complexity. In *patidar*-dominated Charotar, the Baraiyas were mostly poor peasants or labourers, but there were neighbouring areas where most substantial peasants were Baraiyas. The caste-class link was strong at the village level, much less so for the district as a whole, but "peasants tended to perceive their interests at that level, as at the village level, in terms of caste rather than class".[113]

As sociologists have often pointed out, the kind of 'modernization' we have had so far in our country has on the whole strengthened rather than weakened fragmentation and conflicts along caste lines.[114] Improved communications facilitated wider, 'horizontal' combinations (while weakening local 'vertical' ties of *jajmani* dependence); English education provided a new ladder to social promotion for small but growing minorities; colonial economic exploitation involved a process of differentiation which benefited some Indians at the expense of others; and Census attempts from 1901 to classify castes on the basis of recognized social precedence led to a flood of claims and counter-claims as *jati* leaders jostled for pre-eminence, organized caste associations, and invented mythological caste 'histories'. Successful leading members of a *jati* found it useful to mobilize support from caste-brethren in their usually quite parochial and selfish struggle for social recognition, jobs, and, increasingly, political status. This process was greatly stimulated by the gradual introduction of electoral politics from the 1880s onwards. As for the poorer members of a *jati*, patronage links with more successful fellow-members seemed often the only road for survival in an increasingly competitive, harsh, and alien world. It must be added that *jatis* low down the social scale tend to be particularly jealous of their superiority vis-a-vis groups still lower down, leading to the world of Indian toilers becoming fragmented to an unusual extent. Movements inspired by broader ideologies, either national or class, could render such things secondary; but traditional barriers subsumed in a flood of mass enthusiasm could recur with the return to 'normalcy', making ideologies take second place to considerations of factional and caste politics.

The phenomenon of 'caste movements', which became an increasingly important part of the Indian social and political scene from about the turn of the century onwards, has been sought to be interpreted in at least three ways. They have been accepted, more or less at their face value, as modern expressions of the upward mobility through Sanskritization of particular *jatis* as a whole; denigrated, predictably, by the 'Cambridge school' as mere factional manouvres of patron-client linkages whose claims to represent their caste were as flimsy and unacceptable as nationalist efforts to speak for the whole country; and considered, as notably by Gail Omvedt in her study of the Maharashtra non-Brahman movement, as distorted but important expressions of class tensions which might at times go radically beyond the Sanskritization model of mere 'positional mobility'. The variations in approach are perhaps not unnatural, for caste movements have differed considerably in composition and objectives alike. Among lower castes, for example, the Chamars of Jaunpur investigated by Bernard Cohn with their cult of Siva Narayana and imitation of Brahmanical forms,[115] or the mercantile upper stratum of the Shanar untouchable caste of toddy tappers and agricultural labourers in south Tamilnad who began calling themselves Nadars and asserting temple-entry rights,[116] fit in fairly well into a frame of analysis which emphasizes Sanskritizing claims to higher ritual status, accompanied or followed by more 'secular' demands for better job opportunities. The real benefits in such movements remain confined in the main to an upper crust within the *jati*: the emergence of prosperous Nadar merchants has hardly improved the lot of the Shanar toddy-tappers of Tirunelveli. The Mahar movement of Maharashtra began in the 1890s with similar claims to Kshatriya origin, but under Ambedkar's leadership, it developed from the 1920s into a real attack on the caste system, with militant temple-entry campaigns, public burning of *Manusmriti*, some connections with the Bombay labour movement, and eventually conversion to Buddhism.[117] The Ezhava awakening in Kerala started under the religious leader Sri Naryana Guru and his SNDP-Yogam (1902-03), attacking upper caste domination and demanding temple-entry; some of its leaders, like C. Kesavan and K. Aiyyappan, turned towards atheism in the 1930s, and inspired many to take the road towards the Communist Party.[118]

A similar diversity characterized movements among intermediate or upper castes. The Kayasthas with their lead in English education and countrywide linkages through the professions were, not unnaturally, the first caste movement to develop all-India pretensions, with a conference in Lucknow attended by delegates from Bengal, Bihar, UP, and Bombay as early as 1887. The change they were primarily interested in was correspondingly modest—recognition of 'twice-born' status.[119] Sanskritizing efforts and claims to better job opportunities were the principal staples also of the Mahishya movement in Midnapur, consisting of a section of the Kaivartas claiming a new nomenclature and higher status, under the leadership of some zamindars and a few Calcutta-based lawyers and traders. For the Goala or Yadavs of Patna, Monghyr, Darbhanga anal Muzaffarpur villages challenging upper caste domination in the 1920s, however, demands for educational opportunities and higher ritual status were accompanied by movements "not to do *begari* for zamindars... pari passu with taking the sacred thread they have been proposing to refuse menial and other services hitherto rendered to their landlords".[120] In Madras Presidency, the Justice Party challenge to Brahman domination of the professions (3 per cent of the population, but 70 per cent of the graduates between 1870-1918) was essentially the movement of a counter-elite among non-

Brahman caste Hindus (Vellala, Reddi, Kamma, Nayar) led by prosperous landlords and merchants.[121] The Dravidian or Tamil ideology did acquire, however, a much more radical and populist dimension in the 1920s through E.V. Ramaswami Naickar's Self-Respect movement.[122] A similar dualism emerges from Gail Omvedt's analysis of the Non-Brahman movement in Maharashtra spearheaded by Jyotiba Phule's Satyashodhak Samaj, a moderate 'Sanskritizing' trend, interested only in Kshatriya status and more jobs for the elite among the Maratha caste-cluster (and as loyalist as their Justice counterparts in Madras); but also a much more radical, anti-caste, and village-based movement under leaders like Mukundrao Patil, claiming to speak for the *bahujan samaj* against *Shetji-bhatji* domination, and spreading its message through vernacular tracts and folk *tamashas.*[123] It is interesting that both the Self-Respect and the Satyashodhak movements attempted inversions of the *Ramayana* myth, glorifying Ravana against Rama in Tamilnad and reviving an old peasant cult of Bali-Raj slain by Sugrib and Rama in Maharashtra.

Reacting against communalist historiography, Indian nationalist and Marxist scholarship has tended to explain Hindu-Muslim conflicts either in terms of British divide-and-rule combined with elite squabbles, or through a somewhat simplistic economic, reductionism (e.g. Muslim peasants facing Hindu gentry in East Bengal and Malabar, or Hindu traders in the Punjab). A better understanding of the more 'populist' brands of Muslim or Hindu communalism (which, unfortunately, did have a certain autonomous existence) may be reached perhaps through a pattern of analysis similar to the one suggested for caste problems.

Once again, congruence and asymmetry coexisted in the class-religious community relationship, simultaneously permitting expression of socio-economic grievances through a religious idiom, and blurring class division. Thus the familiar Muslim peasantry-Hindu landlord explanation of

East Bengal communalism probably requires some qualification, for Muslim rent-receivers in fact outnumbered upper-caste Hindus in the Rajshahi and Chittagong divisions.[124] But most big zamindars (and trader-moneylenders) were Hindus, and Muslim peasants tended increasingly to look up to the successful minority within their community as leaders, developing connections with this upper crust–through peasant sons becoming *mullahs*, for instance. A simple class-religion identity is clearly even less relevant in Bihar or the United Provinces, though such relationships may well have been decisive at the micro-level (e.g. Muslim artisans and Hindu merchants in towns, Hindu peasants and Muslim *talukdars* in parts of Awadh, a predominantly. Hindu countryside vs towns partly dominated by Muslims, etc.).

Through a pioneering study of a mass of Bengali *puthi* literature, Rafiuddin Ahmed has recently established the existence of a strong sectional consciousness among rural Muslims nearly a generation before organized elite communalism became a significant force in Bengal.[125] For the better understanding of mass nationalism and communalism alike, we urgently need more such studies of cheap vernacular tracts, akin to the broadsides and cheapbooks which have been used to illuminate the world of popular culture in early modern Europe,[126] though it is important to remember Carlo Ginzburg's warning about the need to distinguish "culture *produced by*" from "culture *imposed on* the popular classes".[127] In the absence of such studies, a lot remains mysterious about manifestations of popular communalism like the cow-slaughter riots of the early 1890s or the massive Shahabad explosion of October 1917. Gaurakshini Sabhas fostered by some zamindars and lawyers had become active in many parts of Northern India from the 1880s. But really organized elite Hindu or Muslim communalism still lay in the future when riots ravaged large parts of eastern UP and Bihar and spread to Bombay in the summer of 1893. And in 1917 relations between Hindu and Muslim political leaders were unusually friendly in the wake of the Lucknow Pact. Again, unlike the anti-zamindar-*mahajan* outbursts, in Comilla and Mymensingh in 1906-07, the beginnings of the Praja movement with the Kamariarchar conference in 1914 formulating rich peasant demands but under a specifically Muslim leadership,[128] or the Calcutta riots of September 1918 where the principal targets were Burra Bazar Marwari businessmen,[129] clear economic roots are much more difficult to trace for riots over cow-slaughter or on the music-before-mosque issue. What requires particular emphasis in the context of the present discussion is the extremely volatile nature of popular sentiments and movements. In Shahabad district in October 1917, for instance, the immediate issue was cow-protection, but crowds of upto 50,000 Hindu peasants attacking Muslim villages seem to have been influenced by widespread rumours that British rule was collapsing. Rioting crowds shouted *'Angrez ka raj uthh gaya'* and even *'German ki jay'*; and the area affected coincided with what had been Kunwar Singh's base in 1857-58.[130] To take another example, Inder Narayan Dwivedi was a Sanatan Dharma Sabha activist and protege of Malaviya, who combined propagation of Hindi with Home Rule politics and the starting of Kisan Sabhas in 1917 in the Allahabad region.[131] At both 'elite' and 'popular' levels, both Hindu revivalism and its rough Muslim counterpart, Pan-Islamism, could oscillate between expression of material discontent, communal frenzy, and anti-imperialist politics.

This may be the appropriate place to attempt a preliminary stocktaking of the significance and limits of popular movements in more general terms. The pre-First World War era is really in a way more suited than the Gandhian phase for such an evaluation, for the movements we have been considering so far were essentially 'spontaneous' and no more than marginally affected by intelligentsia ideologies, objectives or techniques. The limitations of such 'spontaneity' are fairly clear. Popular movements were directed usually against the immediate Indian oppressor rather than the distant white superior, and so were often not consciously or subjectively anti-imperialist. They tended to be fairly widely scattered in both space and time, and were extremely volatile, with class, caste and religious forms of articulation interpenetrating and passing over into each other with bewildering ease. All this makes it rather difficult to accept without some qualification the concept of 'peasant nationalism' as a coherent alternative to elite patriotic ideologies and movements. Popular initiative and autonomy were undoubted, even remarkable at times, but, unlike middle class nationalism which does have a certain continuity, at the level of ideology at least, from the formulation of the drain of wealth theory in the 1870s onwards, the movements we have been considering were clearly far more fragmented.

Yet despite such limitations and crudities, popular unrest did anticipate much of middle class nationalism in terms of issues and forms of struggle, while its specific gains were at times not inconsiderable. Forest rights, the burdens of rent, usury and land revenue, planter exploitation, and labour grievances were all themes which were taken up by the mainstream of middle class nationalism very much later, and that incompletely. In 1890, when Moderate Congress politics of "mendicancy" seemed to be the only kind of Indian nationalism, a Bombay Governor was writing to the Viceroy:

> The forest policy, the *Abkari* policy, the Salt duty, the screwing up of land revenue by revision settlements, all make us odious... We know pretty well what the educated natives want, but what the feelings are of the uneducated, I admit I don't know.[132]

Forty years later, Gandhi would forge an all-India movement precisely around the issues of salt and land revenue, excise and forest rights. The anticipations at the level of forms of struggle were equally remarkable; collective refusals of rent or revenue, accompanied at times by *hizrats;* social boycott; the *hartal* and the *dharmaghat;* as well as forms like food riots, social banditry, millenarian hopes, terroristic actions, and mass insurrection, which 'official' nationalism never accepted but which still contributed considerably at times to anti-imperialist movements. And popular outbreaks did bring certain definite gains, special administrative arrangements restricting *diku* encroachments in many tribal areas; the decline of indigo in Bengal after 1859-60; consolidation of occupancy rights for sections of the Bengal peasantry; anti-moneylender legislation in the Maharashtra Deccan and elsewhere; special regulations protecting *khuntkatti* tenure after Birsa Munda's robellion; gradual relaxation of revenue pressures. The British, of course, did their best, at times successfully, to absorb such concessions into the overall colonial structure and use them to buttress it through methods of divide and rule, but a similar statement could be made about concessions given under middle class pressure like the successive homeopathic doses of Council reform. One might even argue that elite nationalism before Gandhi perhaps achieved less in terms of specific gains: for instance it took more than a generation to win the demand for simultaneous ICS examinations, and the countervailing excise against Indian textiles was lifted only in 1925 in the context of a Bombay labour strike.

The theoretical statement, grounded in Lenin and possibly Marx, that 'subaltern', particularly peasant, movements to become really effective require organization and ideology coming in large part from outside and above, does have a certain validity: twentieth century peasant wars have generally succeeded only under leaderships transcending purely peasant aims.[133] But a leap is sometimes made from this general proposition to a quite different, more specific, and much more dubious one: that the Indian colonial middle class was able to supply this necessary ideology and organization and thus, eventually, establish a full-scale 'hegemony'.

Space does not permit more than a very brief discussion of the nature and limits of what may be schematically presented as the four main contributions of the nineteenth century middle class to Indian life: religious and social reform, patriotic literature, the economic critique of British rule, and modern political organization culminating in the Indian National Congress. The obvious and basic contradiction here was between broadly bourgeois ideals and self-image as a *madhyabitta sreni* derived from a growing awareness of contemporary developments in the West, and a predominantly non-bourgeois social base in the professions dependent on English education combined with various types of rentier interests (zamindari or intermediate tenures in the Permanent Settlement areas, petty landlordism elsewhere).[134] The characteristic alienation of an 'enlightened', reforming intelligentsia from the masses was compounded here by the foreign medium of modern education.

While intelligentsia reform movements did emphasize a largely new and very valuable note of rationality, and make some contributions in specific fields like the women's question, they failed to really overcome the basic barriers fragmenting Indian society: caste and religion. Thus a concept of 'Muslim tyranny' during a 'medieval' dark age (from which British rule with its accompanying alleged 'renaissance' or 'awakening' had been a deliverance) is to be found in Rammohun and among Derozians almost as much as in Bankimchandra,[135] and the theoretically anti-caste Brahmo movement confined its programme on that plane mainly to more or less symbolic actions.[136] In any case, 'reform' by the late nineteenth century was being largely swamped by numerous varieties of Hindu 'revival', and while nationalists like Tilak, Bipin Pal or Aurobindo felt that this could be an easy way to mobilize the masses, the partial alliance of Extremism with revivalism in the end sharpened

Muslim alienation and also aroused lower-caste suspicions (e.g. in Madras and Maharashtra).

National, regional, caste, and communal consciousness in fact interpenetrated and intermingled with each other as much, if not more, at the level of middle class thought and action as in popular movements. Thus the specifically modern forms of nationalism and communalism emerged at about the same time (around the last quarter of the nineteenth century), had similar social roots,[137] and were sometimes even combined, in varying proportions, within the same individuals. The same ambiguities are vividly reflected in the patriotic literature developing in regions like Bengal and Maharashtra from the 1860s onwards.

The systematic economic critique of British rule was by far the most solid achievement of the Moderate generation. Though what may for convenience be characterized as the drain of wealth ideology did have serious limitations,[138] it was still much less of a 'false consciousness' than movements which had sought a solution for the country's sorrows through social reform, revivalism, communal or caste alignments, or regional loyalties. One significant achievement of the Extremist phase was the popularization of this economic critique, and here it would be appropriate to mention the name of Sakharam Ganesh Deuskar, whose *Desher Katha* (four editions in 10,000 copies between 1904 and 1907) expounded in eloquent but simple Bengali the arguments of Dadabhai Naoroji and R.C. Dutt. But in its eagerness to slur over the tensions within Indian society, nationalist economic theory kept largely silent over exploitation by Indian landlords, moneylenders, traders, or industrialists, and hence had relatively little to offer in concrete terms to many subaltern groups—a theoretical limitation which would continue to have its counterpart in practice virtually throughout the history of the national movement.

If moderate politics could be characterized without serious injustice as ineffective and 'mendicant', the Swadeshi period in Bengal, Maharashtra and Punjab did develop a whole new range of political techniques, many of them clearly anticipating Gandhian forms: boycott, Swadeshi enterprise, national schools, passive resistance. But in practice 'constructive Swadeshi' and forms of mass mobilization soon withered away, leaving mendicant 'agitation' and individual terrorism as opposite poles united on a common base of elite action: a shift from the one to the other was really much easier and socially less dangerous than a breakthrough towards genuine mass action. Mclane has emphasized the elitist lifestyle and consequent social inhibitions of the Moderate leadership, producing feelings of mingled contempt and fear of the 'lower orders'. Pherozeshah Mehta travelled in a special railway saloon, a Congress leader asked Gandhi to button his shirt for him during the 1901 session, Dinshaw Wacha recalled the blowing of 1857 rebels from British guns without the slightest sympathy in his *Shells from the Sands of Bombay*, and Surendranath Banerji during a temperance campaign in 1887 found the lower classes utterly alien.[139] Extremist leaders despite their rhetoric were hardly very different in their way of life and attitudes, and the urban professional intelligentsia in general had close connections with propertied groups: a few industrialists in Bombay, commercial magnates like the Tandons of Allahabad,[140] rent-receivers practically everywhere. Aurobindo even in his most radical mood shied away from any call for no-revenue or no rent, the one really effective form of passive resistance in a peasant country, while the marked lack of enthusiasm among the bourgeoisie proper (as distinct from intellectuals with bourgeois aspirations) robbed boycott and Swadeshi of much of its force. Boycott of British goods in Swadeshi Bengal had to be attempted through student picketing of shops and social boycott of recalcitrant merchants, the collective trader vows which would characterize post-1920 boycotts being still significantly absent. The real spread of nationalist politics beyond the confines of the intelligentsia to business groups and peasants alike had to wait for the post-War era and Gandhi.

NOTES

1. Eric Stokes, "Traditional Resistance Movements and Afro-Asian Nationalism: The Context of the 1857 Mutiny rebellion in India" (*Past and Present*, No. 48, August 1970), reprinted in his *The Peasant and the Raj: Studies in Agrarian Society and Peasant Rebellion in Colonial India* (Cambridge, 1978); K. Suresh Singh, *Colonial Transformation of the Tribal Society in Middle India* (Proceedings of Indian History Congress, Bhubaneswar session, 1977). For an introductory survey of African developments, see Basil Davidson, *Africa in Modern History* (Pelican, 1978).
2. Kathleen Gough has used the category 'restorative' to describe this type of resistance. "Indian Peasant Uprisings", *Economic and Political Weekly*, Special Number, August 1974.
3. S.B. Chaudhuri, *Civil Disturbances during British Rule in India, 1765-1857* (Calcutta, 1953).
4. Upto February 1859, the British had seized in Awadh 4,27,939 swords, 29,941 spears, 6,418 bows and arrows, and 1,29,414 firearms. Rudrangshu Mukherjee, *The Rebellion in Awadh, 1857-58: A Study in Popular Resistance* (unpublished D. Phil. thesis, Oxford, 1981), pp. 237, 245 and *passim.*
5. T. Metcalf, *Land, Landlords and the British Raj: Northern India in the Ninteenth Century* (California, 1979), *passim.*
6. S.T. Jassal, "Agrarian Contradictions and Resistance in Faizabad District of Oudh", *Journal of Peasant Studies*, Vol. 7, No. 3, April 1980, pp. 312-337.
7. The standard account of peasant-cum-zamindar resistance in Mughal India remains Irfan Habib's, *Agrarian System of Mughal India* (Bombay; 1963), Chapter IX; but see also Gautam Bhadra, "Mughal Yuge Krishak-Bidroha—Ekti Prathamik Ruparekha," *Ekshan*, Volume XIII, n. 5-6, 1385/1978, as well as Irfan Habib's recent paper, "Forms of Class Struggle in Mughal India", Indian History Congress, Bombay, 1980.

8. See for example the account of the rising of the Croquants of Perigord (1637) against tax farmers, and that of the 'Nu-pieds' of Normandy (1639) against Richelieu's efforts to stamp out local salt production in the interests of the state salt monopoly —R. Mousnier, *Peasant Uprisings in 17th Century France, Russia and China* (London, 1971). The Porshnev-Mousnier controversy regarding the nature of 17th century French peasant movements deserves greater attention from our medievalists: See Gately, Moote, Wills, "Seventeenth Century Peasant Furies: Some Problems of Comparative History" (*Past and Present*, No. 51, May 1971); and P.J. Coveney (ed.), *France in Crisis, 1620-1675* (London, 1977). Ladurie has also distinguished between two basic types of peasant rebellion, anti-noble and anti-tax. See *Carnival*, Chapter 13.
9. D.A. Washbrook, "Law, State, and Society in Colonial India", in C. Baker, G. Johnson, and A. Seal (eds.), *Power, Profit and Politics* (Cambridge, 1981), p. 671.
10. R.P. Dutt, *India Today* (2nd edition, Bombay, 1947), p. 198, and S.J. Patel, *Agricultural Labourers in Modern India and Pakistan* (Bombay, 1952), *passim.*
11. Dharma Kumar, *Land and Caste in South India: Agricultural Labour in the Madras Presidency during the 19th Century.* (Cambridge, 1965), Chapters III, XI.
12. "At the bottom there was the landless proletariat created in Mughal India, not by capitalism but by an age-old operation of the caste system for the benefit of peasant agriculture. There are, perhaps, few parallels in the world when the oppressors and the oppressed majority in society have joined together to keep a minority in such utter degradation for their own advantage". Habib, "Forms of Class Struggle in Mughal India", pp. 5-6.
13. T. Shanin, *The Awkward Class: Political Sociology of Peasantry in a Developing Society: Russia 1910-1925* (Oxford, 1972), offers a detailed explication of the ideas of the Chayanov school; see also the criticisms of Shanin in *Journal of Peasant Studies*, Volume VII (1979).
14. See particularly, out of a fascinating and growing literature,

E.J. Hobsbawm, *Primitive Rebels* (Manchester, 1959) and *Bandits* (Pelican, 1972); G. Rude, *Crowd in History 1730-1848* (New York, 1964), and his "Pre-Industrial Crowd" reprinted in *Paris and London in the 18th Century: Studies in Popular Protest* (Fontana, 1970); E.P. Thompson, "The Moral Economy of the English Crowd", *Past and Present,* No. 50, 1971, and *Whigs and Hunters* (Allen Lane,1975); D. Hay *et al,* (ed.), *Albion's Fatal Tree: Crime and Society in 18th Century England* (Allen Lane, 1975); and V.A.C. Gatrell, *et al,* (ed.), *Crime and the Law: The Social History of Crime in Western Europe Since 1500* (London, 1980).

15. David Arnold, "Dacoity and Rural Crime in Madras, 1860-1940", *Journal of Peasant Studies,* January, 1979.
16. Ravinder Kumar, "Bombay Textile Strike, 1919" *Indian Economic and Social History Review,* March 1971; David Arnold, "Looting, Grain Riots, and Government Polity in South India, 1918", *Past and Present,* August, 1979; and Rajat Roy, *Social Conflict and Political Unrest in Bengal, 1875-1927* (unpublished Cambridge Ph.D. thesis).
17. See p. 51.
18. Alauddin Khalji's price fixation is always presented as something more or less unique. See for example, W.H. Moreland, *Agrarian System of Moslem India* 1929, Chapter II. The absence of price controls (or of a just price religious ethic) need not imply, however, the prevalence of a free market situation of the modern type; quite possibly it might indicate rather the relative unimportance of the market for rural consumers as compared to conditions in early modern Europe, given the existence of traditionally-fixed non-market exchange of products between peasants and artisans in the *jajmani* system and the absence of rural demand for urban goods due to the massive pumping away of peasant surplus through land revenue. See Irfan Habib's comments on the coexistence of commodity production with rural self-sufficiency in Mughal India. *Agrarian System,* pp. 118-19.
19. Arnold, "Dacoity and Rural Crime"; Hobsbawm, *Bandits,* p. 20.

20. Hardiman, *Peasant Nationalists,* pp. 47, 265.
21. Arnold mentions in this context the Lambadi itinerant traders ousted by railways, the Maravars and Kallars who lost their traditional livelihood as village watchmen under British rule, and tribals of the Gudem region in Andhra among whom dacoity spread as shifting cultivation was banned in the forest. For forest 'crimes', see pp. 10-16.
22. Crooke and Enthoven, *Religion and Folklore of Northern India* (1925), p. 180.
23. "The Son", and "Bhimo Jat–the Outlaw", in Tara Bose, *Folk Tales of Gujarat* (New Delhi, 1971).
24. Hardiman, *Peasant Nationalists,* pp. 164-65.
25. S.J. Hobsbawm, *Primitive Rebels,* p. 24.
26. For millenarianism in general, see Hobsbawm, *Primitive Rebels:* C. Hill, *The World Turned Upside Down* (Penguin, 1975); N. Cohn, *The Pursuit of the Millennium* (London, 1970); P. Worsley, *The Trumpet Shall Sound* (Paladin, 1970); V. Lantemari, *The Religions of the Oppressed* (London, 1963); and S. Trupp, (ed.), *Millennial Dreams in Action,* in *Comparative Studies in Society and History,* 1962. The only full-length Indian study so far, by no means very satisfactory, is Stephen Fuchs, *Rebellious Prophets: A Study of Messianic Movements in Indian Religions* (Bombay, 1965).
27. See for example, an official analysis of the causes of the major tribal rebellion under Alluri Sitarama Raju in 1922-1924: in the Godavari forest "Some [of the rebels] had been fined what appeared to be unnecessarily large sums for forest offences and resented not being able to go into the forest and cut what they wanted for their ordinary purposes or to graze even young calves without fee.... Others who had no lands nor cattle said they had been able to eke out their living by *podu* before it was restricted. *Podu* does seem to have been the resource ...also to some extent of the men with lands because they have not enough cattle to properly manure and cultivate the valley kind...". Special Commissioner, Agency Operations, to Madras Chief Secretary, 22 August 1924. M. Venkatarangaiyya (ed.), *Freedom Struggle in Andhra Pradesh,* Volume III (Hyderabad, 1965), p. 368.

28. For comparable situations in medieval Europe and eighteenth century England, see R. Hilton, *Bondmen Made Free: Medieval Peasant Movements and the English Rising of 1381* (London, 1977), pp. 40, 70-71; and Thompson, *Whigs and Hunters, passim.* The fourth and fifth articles of the famous Twelve Articles of the German peasant rebels of 1525 also denounced restrictions on hunting, fishing, and appropriation of timber in the forests. See appendix to F. Engels, *Peasant War in Germany* (1874) in K. Marx, *Historical Writings*, Volume II (Bombay, 1945), p. 739. The theme of alienation of forests seem really world-wide. See the reminiscences of Karari Njama, Mau Mau leader, about a childhood conversation with his grandfather: "Today we are forbidden to collect firewood from that forest which was ours; we are not allowed to cut even strings for tying together wood when building a but". D.L. Barrett and Karari Njama, *Mau Mau from Within* (New York, 1970), p. 86.
29. D.D. Kosambi, *Culture and Civilization of Ancient India in Historical Outline* (London, 1965), p. 34.
30. W.G. Archer, *The Hill of Flutes* (Pittsburg, 1974), pp. 23-24 has a deeply moving passage on the continuing manifold significance of forests to Santals in the Dumka region, settled agriculturists for whom the hunt had become no more than an annual ritual: "[The forests] supply the villagers with twigs and branches for fuel, timber for rafters and tools, and leaves for plates and cups:.. If the year is bad, the forest is scoured for roots, leaves and berries ...But above all, the forest is a place for secret recreation.... The beat may nowadays yield only a hare or a peacock...but an aura of faint romantic danger persists... At the greatest occasion of all... the annual hunt they assemble from far and near, spend the day scouring the hillsides and uplands and then at night debate tribal matters and regale themselves with 'music hall entertainments'.... Finally, the forest is a trysting-place for lovers...".
31. An alternation noted as characteristic of millenarian movements by Hobsbawm in his *Primitive Rebels* (3rd edition)

p. XI, and analysed in much greater detail in Worsley's *The Trumpet Shall Sound,* a fascinating study of Melanesian cargo-cults.

32. Stephen Fuchs, *Rebellious Prophets,* pp. 54-56; J. Macdougall, "Agrarian Reform versus Religious Revitalization: Collective Resistance to Peasantization among the Mundas, Orans and Santals, 1858-95". *Contributions to Indian Sociology,* Vol. II, No. 2 (New Series), 1977.
33. This seems to be a recurrent belief in folk rebellions. See p. 15.
34. K. Suresh Singh, *The Dust Storm and the Hanging Mist: A Study of Birsa Munda and His Movement in Chotanagpur 1874-1901* (Calcutta, 1966), pp. 27-30, 33-37, 87-90, 180-85. The earlier, pioneering work of Sarat C. Roy, *Tile Mundas and Their Country* (1912) remains useful for Munda agrarian and social structure.
35. Stephen Fuchs, *Rebellious Prophets,* pp. 36-44.
36. *Ibid.,* pp. 218-22.
37. *Ibid.,* pp. 242-43. A fuller account is in Government of India, Home Police B December 1913 n 108-117. For the battle on 'Sail Rakab hill, see K. Suresh Singh, *Dust Storm,* pp. 109ff.
38. Stephen Fuchs, *Rebellious Prophets,* pp. 148-49. For the importance in European popular culture of similar cults of 'sleeping heroes', see Peter Burke, *Popular Culture in Early Modern Europe* (London, 1978), pp. 152-53.
39. Gautam Bhadra, "The Kuki (?) Uprising (1917-19): Its Causes and Nature", *Man in India* (March 1975).

39a. A detailed study of the tribal movements in this area was published just after the completion of this paper. See D. Arnold, "Rebellious Hillmen: The Gudem Rampa Risings, 1839-1924" in R. Guha (ed.), *Subaltern Studies 1.*

40. F.R. Hemingway (ed.), *Godavari District Gazetteer* (Madras, 1907), p. 272.
41. *Ibid*: see W. Francis (ed.), *Vizagapatam District Gazetteer* (Madras, 1907), which states that the rebel leader Tamma Dom was hailed as Raja of south Malkangiri; and also Government of Madras to Secretary of State, 25 August 1879, which reports efforts by insurgents "to obtain support from the Bastar territory". GOI Home Police B September 1879 n 23.

42. H.E. Sullivan's Report to Government of Madras, No. 111C, 27 September 1879; Home Judicial B February 1880 n 208-209.
43. Deposition of prisoner Karam Potti Dora: Home Judicial B October 1879 n 123-125.
44. Sullivan's Report, *loc.cit.*
45. "They have been carrying on this 'podu' cultivation for ages, and what is the result? There still remains an unbroken tract of almost impenetrable forest covering an area of 5000 square miles." The Godavari Collector, however, felt that restrictions were necessary to develop prospects of teak cultivation in the future. Other forest grievances in Rekapalle were the new tax per acre of cleared forest in place of the previous tax per axe (which immediately tripled the burden, according to Sullivan's calculations), and the need to obtain licenses from *tahsil* headquarters 30-40 miles away in Bhadrachalam. *Ibid*; also report of J.L. Loch, 26 November 1879 in Home Police A January 1880 n 77-80.
46. Low-country, traders bought up tamarind fruits from the tribals, and frequently swindled them of their land through connections with the Rajahmundry court. As elsewhere, the totally unfamiliar British legal system proved a major source of oppression for tribals. Sullivan, *op. cit.* See also the statements of Pusem Chinnaya Dora, who lost all his cattle (worth Rs. 160) for failing to repay a debt of Rs. 5 (the trader "brought a suit; that is, he brought a gumastah and said he had brought a suit"), and of the *muttadar* of Berampalli, brought under the control of a Komati trader through indebtedness: Home Judicial B February 1880 n 208-209, Appendix III.
47. Depositions of Kamm Potti Dora and Kamm Gangadu: Home Judicial B October 1879 n 123-125.
48. Hemingway, *Godavari District Gazetteer*.
49. Report of J.L. Loch : Home Police A January 1880 n 77-80.
50. The concessions were approved by the Secretary of State in his despatch to the Madras Governor-in-Council, 6 May 1880 —Home Police B June 1880 n 12. See also Hemingway, *op. cit.*, pp. 93-96, 276.

51. Quoted in David Arnold, "Dacoity and Rural Crime", p. 162.
52. E. Thurston and K. Rangachari, *Castes and Tribes of South India*, Volume III (Madras, 1909), pp. 350-353.
53. Hemingway, *Godavari District Gazetteer*, pp. 92-101.
54. Thurston and Rangachari, *Castes and Tribes*, Volume II, p. 32.
55. E. Clemant Smith, "The Baster Rebellion (1910)". This is an account by a British soldier fighting the revolt, published in *Man in India*, Rebellion Number, December 1945.
56. Home Police B, March 1915, n 153.
57. Conrad Wood, "Peasant Revolt: An Interpretation of Moplah Violence in the 19th and 20th Centuries", in Dewey and Hopkins (ed.), *The Imperial Impact* (London, 1978).
58. Stephen F. Dale, *Islamic Society on the South Asian Frontier: The Mappilas of Malabar, 1498-1922* (Oxford, 1980), p. 123.
59. See *Ibid.*, pp. 228-32, for a very interesting table listing the date, location; and social composition of the victims and their Mappila assailants in the 32 incidents between 1836 and 1919.
60. Wood, *op. cit.*
61. Tilly, *The Vendee*, Chapter V. Margadant also relates the 'red' and 'white' belts of mid-nineteenth century rural France partly to differences in settlement patterns: *French Peasants in Revolt*. Chapter 1.
62. Thus D.H. Dhanagare refers to an increase in the number of Hindu gang robbers between 1865-80: "Agrarian Conflict, Religion and Politics: The Moplah Rebellions in Malabar in the 19th and Early 20th Centuries", *Past and Present*, February 1977.
63. For example, a confrontation at Malappuram mosque with Nayars in 1728, and an attack on the British factory at Tellicherry in 1742. Dale, *Mappilas of Malabar*, Chapters I-III.
64. D.H. Dhanagare, *op. cit.*, Dale, *op. cit.*, p. 201 gives a map showing a decisive concentration of mosques in Ernad and Walavanad.
65. W. Logan, *Malabar Manual*, Volume I (1887; reprinted Madras, 1951), p. 197, notes a 34.63% fall in the number of Cherumars in the decade 1871-81.
66. The Tiruangadi Mappila incident of 1843 sprang out of a

Nayar *jenmi* objecting to a newly-converted Ezhava maid-servant covering her breast and addressing him by the familiar 'you': Dale, *op. cit.*, pp. 130-32.

67. "Our most venerable prophet has said that those who die in battle can see the houris who will come to witness the battle ...Their lips are like coral... their breasts like cups of gold ...they kiss and embrace the martyrs, give them to drink of the sweet water of heaven and gratify their every wish". Quoted in Dale, *Mappilas of Malabar*, p. 133.
68. Carlo Ginzburg, *The Cheese and the Worms: The Cosmos of a 16th Century Miller*, (John Hopkins, 1980), pp. 84-85.
69. W. Logan, *Malabar Manual*, p. 559; Worsley, *The Trumpet Shall Sound, passim.*
70. K. Suresh Singh, *Dust Storm and Hanging Mist*, p. 143.
71. In 1891, 1892, 1893 and 1895: Annie Besant, *How India Wrought for Freedom* (Madras, 1915).
72. This happened at Nagpur in 1896. See J.R. McLane, *Indian Nationalism and the Early Congress* (Princeton, 1977), p. 71. It is significant that Bipan Chandra's voluminous account of early Congress attitudes, to agrarian questions contain no reference to tribal or agricultural labourer grievances. See *Rise and Growth of Economic Nationalism in India* (New Delhi, 1966), pp. 394-496.
73. Government of Bombay, *Source-Materials for a History of the Freedom Movement in India, Volume I: 1818-1885*, (Bombay, 1957).
74. K.K. Sengupta, *Pabna Disturbances and the Politics of Rent, 1873-1885* (New Delhi, 1974), pp. 12-16, 42-45.
75. See. f. n. 56.
76. K.K. Sengupta, *Pabna Disturbances*, p. 44.
77. *Ibid.*, p. 42.
78. An obvious parallel would be the faith in the Tsar as Little Father, shown repeatedly by Russian peasants, and even by Petersburg workers in the demonstration which the Tsar's police shot down on Bloody Sunday, January 1905.
79. K.K. Sengupta, *op. cit.*, pp. 38-39.
80. Thus even Bankimchandra, who had written the strongly

pro-peasant *Bangadesher Krishak* the year before, was moved by stray instances of violence in Pabna to declare that he had been "pained and disgusted by the conduct of the Pabna ryots". *Bangadarsan,* Bhadra B.S. 1280 (1873), cited in *Ibid.,* p. 123.

81. The best discussion of this whole question is in Ashok Sen *Iswarchandra Vidyasagar and His Elusive Milestones* (Calcutta, 1977), pp. 108-121.
82. For a detailed account of the 1906-07 riots, see Sumit Sarkar, *Swadeshi Movement in Bengal, 1903-08* (New Delhi, 1973), Chapter VIII.
83. By 1875, "an amount of grain could be bought for 4 annas which a rupee would hardly have purchased 5 years before." Chief Secretary, Government of Bombay, to Government of India, 6 April 1877: Home Judicial A April 1879 n 3-33.
84. *Ibid.*
85. B.B. Chaudhuri, "Agrarian Economy and Agrarian Relations in Bengal, 1859-1875", in N.K. Sinha (ed), *The History of Bengal 1757-1905* (Calcutta 1967), pp. 265, 280-91.
86. A parallel may perhaps be suggested with the *kulaks* of Russia, often looked up to by their poorer neighbours as "natural leaders" in ways that repeatedly upset Bolshevik calculations in the 1920s. See T. Shanin, *The Awkward Class,* p. 141.
87. Bipan Chandra, *Rise and Growth of Economic Nationalism,* pp. 472-74. Actually there seems to have been little/ correlation between areas severely affected by recent revenue enhancement and the 1875 riots, with the solitary exception of Bhimthari *taluka* in Poona: Home Judicial A April 1879 n 3-33; see also Neil Charlesworth, "Myth of the Deccan Riots of 1875", *Modern Asian Studies,* October, 1972.
88. As Dadabhai Naoroji argued through his concept of 'internal drain', excessive British land taxes, invariably collected in cash, forced peasants to sell more of their produce. This ultimately went out of the country through the British export firms and enhanced the export surplus which was the outward form of the drain of wealth. What this theory largely

ignored, of course, was the subordinate but still quite vital role of India, exploiting groups—zamindars, traders, *mahajans*—in aggravating the burden on the peasant. See B.N. Ganguli, *Dadabhai Nooroji and the Drain Theory* (Asia, 1965), pp. 103-09.

89. Amalendu Guha, *Planter Raj to Swaraj: Freedom Struggles and Electoral Politics in Assam, 1826-1947* (New Delhi, 1977) pp. 50-54.
90. Tilak, we are told by one of his early biographers, "deplored and condemned food riots.... 'Why loot the Bazars', he used to say, 'go to Collector and tell him to give you work and food'." D.V. Athalye, *Life of Lokamanya Tilak* (Poona, 1921), p. 85.
91. McLane, *Early Congress,* pp. 263-64. See also, for the 1896-97 movement, Richard I. Cashman, *The Myth* of *the Lokamanya: Tilak and Mass Politics in Maharashtra* (California, 1975), pp. 126-43.
92. Hardiman, *Peasant Nationalists,* pp. 56-58.
93. N.G. Barrier, "The Punjab Disturbance of 1907: The Response of the British Government in India to Agrarian Unrest", *Modern Asian Studies,* I/4, 1967.
94. "The Sikh and Muslim zamindars wage excited to an intense pitch... Zamindars began to approach me also...I kept putting off [sic] ." Lajpat Rai, *Autobiographical Writings* (ed.), V.C. Joshi (Delhi, 1965), pp. 119-21.
95. Habib, *Agrarian System,* pp. 324-26.
96. Ram Panda, *Agrarian Movement in Rajasthan* (Delhi, n.d.), Chapter 1, provides an unsatisfactory account of a fascinating subject. Hari Sen of Delhi University is now working on a full-length study of Mewar agrarian movements.
97. But for an account emphasizing peasant initiative and the limited nature of the intelligentsia response, see Ranajit Guha, "Neel Darpan: The Image of a Peasant Revolt in a Liberal Mirror", *Journal of Peasant Studies,* October 1974.
98. Girish Mishra, *Agarian Problems of Permanent Settlement: A Case Study of Champaran* (New Delhi, 1978), Chapters 2, 4, 7.
99. Thus agricultural labourers were paid poor wages or made

to do *begar* for indigo planted directly by whites in the *zirat* system which continued as a subsidiary to the more; common *assamiwar* (where tenants were obliged to grow indigo under the *tinkathia* arrangement); Girish Mishra, *Agrarian Problems,* pp. 56-60, 286-92.

100. As distinct from "politicization from the top", through small-town "sub-contractors" employed by Gandhi, as Judith Brown has tried to argue. See Jacques Pouchepadass, "Local Leaders and the Intelligentsia in the Champaran Satyagraha (1917): A Study in Peasant Mobilization" in *Contributions to Indian Sociology,* No. 8 (1974), p. 67.
101. *Ibid.,* p. 73. Pouchepadass also notes the role of some Marwari traders and *mahajans,* who would benefit if peasants grew more foodgrains and sugar cane in place of indigo, and a few local pleaders and school teachers, in organizing the 1917 movement.
102. *Ibid.,* p. 80.
103. Timberg, *The Marwaris* (Delhi, 1978).
104. But in 1844 and 1878 there were also some signs of more unrestrained crowd action. Windows of *sowcar* houses were stoned in 1844 to compel them to join the protest, while "people of anything like a good position were scarce amongst the crowd" in the 1878 demonstrations. Government of Bombay, *Source-Materials for A History of the Freedom Movement in India, Volume I: 1818-1885* (Bombay, 1957), pp. 4-43.
105. E.g., 'union', 'Party', or even 'class' (for which *sreni* or *varna* are at best approximate renderings).
106. The *raiyats,* he complained, "make *Dharma Ghut* or combine *en masse* not to pay rent to the Zamindar". "The Zamindar and the Ryot", *Calcutta Review,* Volume VI, July-December 1846.
107. Report on Kharagpur Strike, from Government of Bengal to Government of India (Home), No. 2141. E.D. of 19 September 1906: Home Public A, December 1906, n 70- 75.
108. Chakrabarty's argument that communal riots among jute labour were perhaps more common than joint anti-employer

class actions has been questioned by Ranajit Dasgupta on the basis of additional data, but the more general point regarding persistence of pre-industrial patterns of consciousness remains a valuable contribution. See Dipesh Chakrabarty, *Communal Riots and Labour: Bengal Jute Millhands in the 1890s* (Centre for Studies in Social Sciences, Calcutta, Occasional Paper No. 11, 1976), and Ranajit Dasgupta, *Material Conditions and Behavioural Aspects of Calcutta Working Class, 1875-99* (CSSSC, Occasional Paper No. 22, 1979).

108a. Sarkar, *Swadeshi Movement,* Chapter V.

108b. Tilak's speeches at labour meetings in the Chinchpoogly industrial area of Bombay concentrated only on boycott of foreign goods and liquor and use of Swadeshi, the latter being advocated on, the argument that through it "the work in the mills would increase and, the employees would be benefited" —Government of Bombay, *Source-Materials* for *a History of the Freedom Movement in India,* Volume II; 1885-1920, (Bombay, 1958), pp. 252-53, 258.

108c. Sarkar, *Swadeshi Movement,* pp. 242-46.

109. Herbert G. Gutman, "Work, Culture and Society in Industrializing America, 1815-1919", *American Historical Review,* June 1973, p. 567.

110. Habib, *Agrarian System,* Chapter IX.

111. E.M.S. Namboodiripad, *National Question in Kerala* (Bombay, 1952), p. 102.

112. H.R. Nevill (ed.), *Rae Bareli District Gazetteer* (Lucknow, 1923), pp. 59-63.

113. Hardiman, *Peasant Nationalists,* pp. 31-36.

114. I am using the term 'caste' throughout in the sense of *jatis,* not of the somewhat abstract and theoretical *varnas.*

115. Bernard Cohn, "Madhopur", in McKion Marriott, (ed.), *Village India: Studies in the Little Community* (Chicago, 1955),

116. R.L. Hardgrave, *The Nadars of Tamilnad* (California, 1969); see also Lloyd and Susanne Rudolph, *The Modernity of Tradition,* Part I (Chicago, 1967).

117. Eleanor Zelliot, "Learning the Use of Political Means: The Mahars of Maharashtra", in Rajni Kothari (ed.), *Caste in Indian*

Politics (Bombay, 1970); Zelliot, "The Leadership of Babasaheb Ambedkar", in B.N. Pandey (ed.), *Leadership in South Asia* (Delhi, 1977).

118. Robin Jeffrey, "Travancore: Status, Class and the Growth of Radical Politics, 1860-1940", in Jeffrey (ed.), *People, Princes and Paramount Power* (OUP, India, 1978).
119. Lucy Carroll, "Swami Shivagan Chand, Kayastha Conference Organizer", *Indian Economic and Social History Review,* July-September, 1975.
120. Bihar Chief Secretary to Government of India (Home), 11 June 1925, quoted in Hetukar Jha, "Lower Caste Peasants and Upper Caste Zamindars in Bihar, 1921-25", *Indian Economic and Social History Review,* October-December, 1977.
121. The Non-Brahman Manifesto of December 1916, for instance, described 'Non Brahmans as constituting "the bulk of the zamindars, landholders, and agriculturists". Eugene Irshchik, *Politics and Social Conflict in South India: The Non-Brahman Movement and Tamil Separatism, 1916-1929* (California, 1969).
122. C.J. Baker, "Leading up to Periyar: The Early Career of E.V. Ramaswami Naicker", in Pandey, *Leadership in South Asia.*
123. Gail Omvedt, *Cultural Revolt in a Colonial Society: The Non-Brahman Movement in Western India, 1873-1930* (Bombay, 1976), Chapters VI-VIII.
124. Partha Chatterjee, Agrarian Relations and Communalism in Bengal, 1926-1935, in R. Guha (ed.), *Subaltern Studies 1,* pp. 10-11.
125. Rafiuddin Ahmed, *The Bengali Muslims, 1871-1906: A Quest for Identity* (OUP, India, 1981).
126. Burke, *Popular Culture,* Part I, 3.
127. Ginzburg, *The Cheese and the Worms,* p. XV.
128. Jatindra Nath De, *History of the Krishak Praja Party in Bengal, 1929-47* (unpublished Ph.D. thesis, Delhi University, 1978). Vernacular pamphlets like *Krishak bandhu* (Calcutta, 1910) clearly reveal the process through which exposure of zamindar-*mahajan* oppression gets transmuted into a call for Islamic solidarity: see my *Swadeshi Movement in Bengal, 1903-1908* (New Delhi, 1973), pp. 462-64.

129. J.H. Broomfield; "The Forgotten Majority: The Bengal Muslims, September, 1918", in D.A. Low (ed.), *Soundings in Modern South Asian History* (California, 1968); K. Mcpherson, *The Muslim Microcosm: Calcutta, 1918 to 1935* (Wiesbaden, 1974), Chapter 3.
130. Peter Robb, "Officials and Non-Officials as Leaders in Popular Agitations: Shahabad 1917 and other 'Conspiracies"', Pandey (ed.), *Leadership in South Asia.* For a recent and more detailed account of the cow-protection riots of 1893 and 1917, see Gyan Pandey, *Rallying Round the Cow: Sectarian Strife in the Bhojpur Region, c 1888-1917* (Centre for Studies in Social Sciences, Calcutta. Occasional Paper No. 39).
131. Majid Siddiqi, *Agrarian Unrest in North India: United Provinces, 1918-1922* (New Delhi, 1978), p. 119.
132. Reay to Lansdowne, 20 February 1890—quoted in B.L. Grover (ed.), *A Documentary Study of British Policy Towards Indian Nationalism* (Delhi, 1967), pp. 141-42. The *Mussalman* of Calcutta made a rather similar comment on 4 October 1907: "The great interest of the six castes [i.e. Brahmans, Kayasths, Vaidyas, Syeds, Mughals, and Pathans] is to get into government service; the great interest of the cultivators is to have salt free and chaukidari tax off and to secure their tenancies". Cited in Rafiuddin Ahmed, *Bengali Muslims,* p. 162.
133. China, Vietnam, Angola and Mozambique would be the obvious examples. For an interesting counter-example of failure of a movement which failed to transcend purely indigenous tribal-peasant forms, see Barrett and Njama, *Mau Mau from Within.*
134. *The Amrita Bazar Patrika* of 9 December 1869 vividly expressed this dualism: 'Middle class (*'madhyabitta'*) people are always considered the most useful group in any society. Our country's welfare depends to a large extent on this class. If there is ever to be a social or any other revolution in this country, it will be by the middle class .... The livelihood of middle class people comes from landed property and the services .... Middle class people are often *gantidars*". [a form

of intermediate tenure common in Jessore, from where the *Amrita Bazar Patrika* was being published at that time].

135. For more details, see my "Rammohun Roy and the Break with the Past", in V.C. Joshi (ed.), *Rammohun Roy and the Process of Modernization in India* (Delhi, 1975), and "Complexities of Young Bengal", *Nineteenth Century Studies*, October, 1973.

136. Like inter-caste marriages among the three upper castes in Bengal, or the insistence that Brahmo *acharyas* give up the sacred thread.

137. The assumption sometimes made that communalists were more 'feudal' than the 'bourgeois' nationalists is hardly tenable in terms of social composition. Examples of zamindari and business patronage may be found in both, and the main bearers of communalist ideology were 'modern' English-educated intellectuals—a Syed Ahmed, a Savarkar, or a Jinnah—rather than traditional *pundits* or *ulema.*

138. Thus concentration on specific 'un-British' official policies (Home Charges, unfair tariffs, excessive revenue burdens, etc.), presumably reversible through the methods of Moderate agitation, led to a relative neglect of the role of private British capital. There was little understanding also of India's vital role in the total imperial economy, and contradictions within Indian society were largely ignored.

139. J.R. McLane, *Indian Nationalism and the Early Congress* (Princeton, 1977), pp. 67-71.

140. Christine Dobbin, *Urban Leadership in Western India: Politics and Communities in Bombay City, 1840-1885* (Oxford, 1972); C. Bayly, *Local Roots of Indian Politics: Allahabad 1880-1920* (Oxford, 1975).

3

1917-1947

The vastly enhanced range of popular movements in the Gandhian era, combined with the fact that much more work has been done on these decades than on the earlier phase, make any attempt at even a relatively comprehensive study both impossible and somewhat unnecessary. Our discussion therefore will be confined to a number of broad problems relating to the varieties of popular movements and the forms of their interaction with middle class leadership.

One may begin with possible explanations of the emergence from 1919 onwards of all-India mass politics—a qualitatively new phenomenon on the whole, though some qualifications may be necessary in terms of partial anticipations of it in a few regions in the 1905-08 period, and of the later ups and downs and uneven regional spread of Gandhian nationalism. The Cambridge interpretation—the Montford reforms by broadening the electorate forced politicians to cultivate a more democratic style—need not detain us very long. It may well explain certain types of politics and politicians,[1] but the most substantial section of Indian politicians did after all boycott elections for some years, and the massive anti-imperialist upsurge of 1919-22 is surely much too big a thing to be explained by a paltry extension of voting rights to between one and three per cent of the adult population. Interpretations of Civil Disobedience and 1942 in terms of the possibility of further constitutional change appear equally trivial.

A basically economic explanation is more attractive and even acceptable—within limits. The First World War, the Depression, and the Second World War all brought about very significant changes in the structure of colonial exploitation, stimulating political action by combining new grievances with growing strength so far as Indian business groups and labour were concerned, and leading to sharp fluctuations in prices which at various times affected adversely all sections of the peasantry. Following the pattern of much recent study of 'long-term trends' in European economic history, it may be tempting also to focus on demography and prices as the two key variables, since the behaviour of both did undergo radical changes after the First World War. Political historians so far have paid relatively little attention to the demographic 'revolution' of the 1920s, which, if Blyn's findings are to be broadly accepted, led not only to stagnation but to actual decline in per capita foodgrains output in the 'Greater Bengal' region in the last decades of the colonial era.[2] Stephen Henningham has recently argued that the acceleration of population growth in North Bihar from 1921 (1881—13.03 millions, 1921—13.82 millions, 1941—16.44 millions) sharpened conflicts overland, worsened conditions of the mass of tenants, and contributed to the conversion of what had been an isolated backwater to a centre of militant agrarian and political movements.[3] As for prices, the post-war inflation, combined with the gap between industrial and agricultural prices, may be related to the distress and discontent among peasants, particularly poorer ones, in the early 1920s; the Depression obviously hit rich and middle peasants hard, stimulating no-revenue and no-rent movements from late 1930; and prices were shooting up again in conditions of wartime scarcity and profiteering on the eve of August 1942.

A closer examination using the tool of comparative

analysis, however, compels certain qualifications. Demographic growth varied very sharply indeed from district to district, and a cursory glance at the United Provinces census data, for instance, reveals how difficult it is to establish any correlation between rapid increase in population and political and/or agrarian militancy. Among districts active in the Kisan Sabha and Non-Cooperation-Khilafat upsurge of the early 1920s, Gorakhpur, Hardoi, and Fyzabad returned a net growth in population for 1881-1931 above the provincial average of + 10.6% (+ 37.2%, + 14.2% + 11.4% respectively). But Allahabad's variation was only +1.2%, and both Pratapgarh with +7.0%, and Rae Bareli with +2.3% the initial base of Baba Ramchandra's Kisan Sabha—returned figures well below the average. Variations in population density may have been somewhat more relevant, with the 'Indo-Gangetic central' districts which were strongholds of the early Kisan Sabha, Non-Cooperation, and Civil Disobedience alike returning density figures considerably higher than the UP average, though even here density was higher still in some regions without organized peasant movements in the early 1920s, in the eastern-most part of the province, for instance.[4] As for prices, the first pressures for no-revenue in Kheda in early 1930 during the Dandi march came several months before Gujarat was at all seriously affected by the Depression,[5] and the scarcity, amounting to devastating famine in Bengal, was obviously far more acute in 1943, when there was no big upheaval, than in the preceding August. Much sharper price-rises (as well as much more intensive demographic growth) have not so far led to comparable all-India protest movements in post-colonial India. The basic assumption behind much economic determinism—that growing misery is a sufficient explanation for popular action—is in fact extremely dubious, and begs the whole complex question as to what kinds of socio-economic situations were most conducive to Gandhian—or non-Gandhian—mass movements.

All this does not imply, of course, that questions of socio-economic structures or conjunctures should or can be ignored. But, as George Lefebvre pointed out in his seminal article, "Revolutionary Crowds", in 1931, the "true causal link" between social, economic, or political "causes" and the "event" or "effects" has to be sought in the formation of a specific "collective frame of mind".[6] And it is in terms of crucial shifts in collective mentalities that it is best to try to understand the phenomenon of Gandhi.

Judith Brown has tried to explain Gandhi's "rise to power"[6a] in term's of skilful political manipulation through "sub-contractors", and it is perfectly true that the Mahatma combined a saintly idiom and apparent quixotry with meticulous and extremely able attention to organizational details. He was helped, somewhat fortuitously, also by certain aspects of his South African career, which gave him not only something of a world reputation but also the possibility of contacts cutting across regions, communities and classes in a manner which was unthinkable for any other Indian politician of the early twentieth century.[7] But the basic fact remains that the impact of Gandhi, particularly during his early years after returning from South Africa, went very far beyond the rather limited ground covered by the organizational network he was gradually building up. The Rowlatt Satyagraha provides an excellent example. H.F. Owen's study reveals the organizational preparation for it to have been quite remarkably patchy and limited. Signatories to the pledge circulated by Gandhi's Satyagraha Sabha, for instance, numbered only 982 in mid-March, 1919—and of these all but 84 came from within Bombay Presidency. Gandhi did undertake a whirlwind countrywide tour, but he never had time to visit the Punjab—the province that was to be most affected.[8] And yet Gandhi cannot be dismissed as irrelevant, for even that most 'un-Gandhian' inflammatory poster in Lahore in April 1919, *Danda Akhbar*, which called on "Hindu, Muhammadan and Sikh brethren [to] fight with bravery against the English monkeys—close offices and workshops...", ended with the assertion: "This is the command of Mahatma Gandhi".[9] Throughout the Gandhian era, the most diverse things would be done in his name. The range, and often the radicalism, of popular actions was remarkable—but so was the irresistible tendency to keep on seeking shelter behind the Mahatma's banner. Both aspects require explanation.

The two features in the Gandhian message which appear most crucial in this context were the implications of *satyagraha*, and Gandhi's apparently rather obscurantist brand of populism. *Ahimsa* and *satyagraha* constituted for Gandhi himself a deeply-felt philosophy of life, but it was fully or sincerely accepted by a relatively small group of disciples. Its application—as a convenient method, rather than a creed—by a decisive section of the Indian political leadership is clearly related to its two-fold impact of drawing in the masses while at the same time keeping mass activity strictly pegged down to certain forms pre-determined by the leader. Indian politicians before Gandhi had tended to oscillate between Moderate mendicancy and individual terrorism basically because of their social inhibitions about uncontrolled mass movements; the *satyagraha* perspective of controlled mass participation now offered a way out of the resultant impasse. The Gandhian model proved acceptable both to business groups, as well as to relatively better-off or locally dominant sections of the peasantry, all of whom stood to lose something if political struggle turned into uninhibited and violent social revolution.

The Gandhian social utopia, put forward most unambiguously in *Hind Swaraj* (1909), was a full scale repudiation of modern industrial civilization. "India's salvation consists in unlearning what she has learnt during the past 50 years or so" for "Railways, lawyers and doctors have impoverished the country ....the so-called upper class have to learn to live consciously and religiously and deliberately the simple life of a peasant".[10] This was undoubtedly unrealistic and even obscurantist if considered as a final remedy for the ills of India or of the world; and it never had much appeal for sophisticated urban groups which by the 1930s and 40s were turning increasingly to either frankly capitalist or socialist solutions, both based on industrialization. But it did represent a reaction to the deeply alienating effects of 'modernization', particularly under colonial conditions.[11] For the artisan ruined by factory industries, the peasant to whom law courts were a disastrous trap and going to a city hospital often an expensive death-sentence, and (particularly, perhaps) for the rural or small town intelligentsia for whom Western education had brought few material benefits and who combined rural connections with a distance from actual work in the fields sufficient to permit idealization of alleged rural harmony, the anti-industrial theme had a real attraction, at least for some time. Gandhi's social ideals were gradually sought to be concretized through programmes of *khadi,* village reconstruction, and (from the 1930s) Harijan welfare. None of these really solved problems in the sense of changing basic social or economic structures. However, tried out with sincerity and patience by devoted Gandhian constructive workers, they could improve to some limited extent the lot of the rural people and, above all, create and sustain stable political bases in the countryside.[12] After the doldrums of the mid-1920s, the salt *satyagraha* of 1930 found its initial cadres and mass support mainly from such *asramas* and constructive work centres.

It must be added that the peasant appeal of Gandhi was greatly helped also by his political style: travelling third class, insisting on the sanctity of manual and even menial work, speaking in simple Hindustani, wearing only loin-cloth from 1921 onwards, and using the imagery of Tulsidas' *Ramayana* so deep-rooted in the popular religion of the North Indian Hindu rural masses. All this marked a sharp break with the style of most Moderate and Extremist politicians alike.

Yet it is fairly obvious that the tremendous breadth of Gandhian movements cannot be explained purely by what Gandhi as a personality actually thought, stood for, or did. What we confront again and again is the crucial role of rumour in a predominantly illiterate society going through a period of acute strains and tensions. From out of their misery and hope—and the years during and just after the War were marked by both, as vague reports filtered in of worldwide revolutionary changes[13]—varied sections of the Indian people seem to have fashioned their own images of Gandhi, particularly in the earlier days when he was still to most people a distant, vaguely glimpsed or heard-of tale of a holy man with miracle-working powers. Thus peasants could imagine that Gandhi would end zamindari exploitation, agricultural labourers of UP dream that "he would provide holdings for them",[14] and Assam coolies leave tea plantations *en masse* in May 1921 saying that they were obeying Gandhi's orders.

A CID report on the *kisan* movement in Allahabad district in January 1921 makes the same point in vivid detail:

> The currency which Mr. Gandhi's name has acquired even in the remotest villages is astonishing. No one seems to know quite who or what he is, but it is an accepted fact that what he says is so, and what he orders must be done .... the real power of his name is perhaps to be traced back to the idea that it was he who got *bedakhli* stopped in Pratapgarh... as a general rule, Gandhi is not thought of as being antagonistic to government, but only to the zamindars...[15]

The process of image-building is fascinating, and deeply ambiguous. Peasants were giving to vague rumours about Gandhi a socially radical, anti-zamindar twist. But at the same time they were attributing their own achievements to him—for, if *bedakhli* (eviction) had been restricted in Pratapgarh, it was due to a peasant struggle under local leaders like Baba Ramchandra, and Gandhi or the Congress leadership had had little or nothing to do with it.[16] If, as would happen repeatedly from 1922, the Mahatma categorically ordered a halt, the bulk of the masses would obey. The peasants still needed to be represented by a saviour from above—a crucial aspect which is perhaps sometimes underestimated. Though hardly, a "sack of potatoes", peasant society was deeply fragmented, and the *Eighteenth Brumaire* of Marx may still have a lot to teach us. Incidentally, the historical necessity for something like a Gandhi-type leadership with strong religious overtones is indicated also by the emergence of a number of somewhat similar regional or local leaders in the early 1920s: Swami Viswananda and Swami Darshanananda among Bengal and Bihar miners, Swami Vidyananda in North Bihar, Baba Ramachandra in eastern UP, Swami Kumarananda in Rajasthan, Ananda Swami in Maharashtra, Alluri Sitarama Raju in the 'Rampa'-Gudem region of Andhra.

The interaction between the specific message and style of the Gandhian leadership and the largely autonomous popular images of Gandhi created complex and varied patterns which recent detailed research has made considerable progress in unravelling. The three themes which stand out are, first, the very considerable role of popular initiative in the unleashing of many of the Gandhian movements; second, the fact that even where a movement began from the top, there was usually a process of radicalization through rumour and the removal by arrest of the 'official' leaders; and third, the role of Gandhian organization as a repeated brake on mass pressures, leading to a peculiar dialectic, first explored by Gyan Pandey, between the strength of the Congress as a party and the extent of more elemental popular initiatives.

The one major exception to this pattern among all-India movements was the anti-War individual civil disobedience of 1940-41, initiated and tightly-controlled by Gandhi throughout—an exception which in a sense proves the rule, for this was also by far the weakest and least effective of all the Gandhian national campaigns. Even here, there is a strong possibility that Gandhi launched this peculiarly limited movement, individual courting of arrest through anti-war speeches, and that not on Sundays, Christmas or before 9 a.m., partly to forestall Socialist and Communist pressures for greater militancy.[17] There was no ground swell in 1940-41, in sharp contrast to what would happen next year. A war which was still a distant affair brought, on the balance, gains rather than losses for substantial sections of the population, through a price-rise, not yet very sharp, which ended a decade of rural depression, a 31 per cent increase in factory employment between 1939 and 1942,[18] and opportunities for lucrative military contracts for businessmen.

Gandhi's first three campaigns on Indian soil were all clearly interventions in movements which had already started. At Champaran his role was limited to holding a public enquiry, while at Kheda the initiative for no-revenue came from local village leaders like Mohanlal Pandya of Kapadvanj *taluka* in November 1917. It was taken up by Gandhi only after considerable hesitation on 22 March 1918, an unwise delay which weakened the case for remissions and made the eventual *satyagraha* a rather patchy affair, involving only 70 villages out of 559.[19] While Non-Cooperation and Civil Disobedience were strategies planned by Gandhi, both were adopted after long periods of pressures from below. One need only recall Gandhi's very moderate stand at the Amritsar Congress of December 1919, and his resistance to the *Purna Swaraj* demand throughout 1928-29. As for the states people's movements, the Gandhian leadership throughout the 1930s showed exceptional hesitation over extending support, probably because these tended to have considerable socially radical potentialities, given the context of near total lack of political rights and rampant feudal oppression of the peasantry. Gandhi openly expressed his displeasure over the AICC resolution of October 1937 calling for solidarity with the Mysore agitation.

Even after Haripura had declared the *Purna Swaraj* ideal to cover the states as much as British India, Gandhi indicated that he would be satisfied if the princes reduced their privy purses and granted a measure of civil liberties and independent courts. Not even responsible government was demanded, far less integration or agrarian reform.[20] The choice of Rajkot for the first personal intervention through *satyagraha* in March 1939 was also very significant: a tiny state surrounded by the firm Gandhian base of Gujarat, almost half its population lived in the capital, and so there was little danger of agrarian radicalism swamping a strictly non-violent *satyagraha*.[21] Much more important movements in the late 1930s—in the Orissan states, Hyderabad, and Travancore, for instance—got no encouragement from the Congress High Command, and Gandhi repeatedly tried to persuade local leaders there to call off the agitations.[22]

Even at Champaran, the psychological impact of Gandhi's intervention far surpassed his concrete activities or intentions. The Bettiah SDO reported on 29 April 1917 that Gandhi "is daily transfiguring the imaginations of masses of ignorant men with visions of an early millennium".[23] A *raiyat* compared Gandhi to Rama, and declared before the enquiry committee that "tenants would not fear the *Rakshasa* —planters now that Gandhi was there". Rumours spread that Gandhi had been sent by the Viceroy or the King to overrule all local officials and planters, and even that the British would leave Champaran soon.[24] The Rowlatt Satyagraha began with a fairly limited programme of volunteers courting arrest through public sale of prohibited works, plus an all-India *hartal* deliberately fixed for a Sunday; it developed into the biggest explosion of mass fury and violence since 1857.

Non-Cooperation-Khilafat again for long was meant to be largely confined to the 'triple boycott' of Councils, courts, and schools, followed up by *Charkha* and boycott of British goods; full scale civil disobedience through no-revenue was repeatedly postponed, and then abandoned, on the very eve of its trial at Bardoli, following the Chauri Chaura incident. Yet apocalyptic rumours of the world turning upside down repeatedly transformed the movement into something very different, and particularly so in regions or among social strata where Gandhian organization was still weak or non-existent. To take a few random examples: forest administration in Palnad and Rayachoti *talukas* of Guntur and Cuddapah virtually collapsed in face of "large bands of men imbued with the idea that Gandhi Raj was either in being or about to be established and that the forest was theirs to work their will upon";[25] there were jail breaks at places like Rajshahi and Trichinopoly, "based on the belief that Gandhi's Swaraj was about to replace British rule";[26] the Khilafat impact set off a massive millenarian revolt among the Mappilas, the bloody suppression of which left 2337 rebels killed, 1652 wounded, and no less than 45,404 prisoners, all mostly from just the two *talukas* of Ernad and Walavanad;[27] Santals attacked police in Jalpaiguri in February 1922, wearing Gandhi caps which they claimed made them immune from bullets; and in the Chaudagram sub-division of Tippera, "no taxes were being paid, and no agricultural rents collected either by government or by private landlords" in the early months of 1922.[28]

A broadly similar pattern of radicalization can also be seen in Civil Disobedience. Though Gandhi initially had called only for a salt *satyagraha,* village officials began resigning their posts all along Gandhi's Dandi march route, and on 19 March 1930 peasants of Ras (in Borsad *taluka* of Kheda) demanded permission for starting immediate non-payment of revenue—a plea which Gandhi accepted with considerable reluctance.[29] Even apart from the eminently non-Gandhian Chittagong Armoury Raid and Peshawar and Sholapur outbursts of April-May 1930, instances of popular peasant or tribal violence multiplied in face of intense repression and arrests of leaders, with crowds fighting back the police, as at Chechuahat in Midnapur in June, to cite one example among many.[30] As agricultural prices crashed, there were mounting pressures also for no-rent, though the Working Committee had sanctioned non-payment of *chaukidari* taxes alone in permanently settled areas in May. The UP provincial leadership did hesitantly accept no-rent in October, the Bihar and Bengal PCCs never formally sanctioned it. The contrast between sanctioned forms of Gandhian agitation and the actual patterns imposed largely through grass-roots initiative is clearest perhaps in the 'forest satyagraha', in Central Provinces, Berar, Maharashtra and Karnataka. The Congress, while taking up tribal and poor peasant grievances about forest restrictions, did its best to restrict the movement to boycott of Forest Department auctions and peaceful mass violations of grazing and timber laws, with the forest produce being publicly sold on the pattern of illegally manufactured salt. But, as at Palnad and Rayachoti in 1921 but on a much larger scale, the actual forest movements often took on forms far more elemental and violent. The Kolis of Kanashi and Chankapur in Nasik district in October, for instance, "filled with stories that the British Raj had been replaced by Gandhi Raj", after a ceremonial banquet "started to shout Congress slogans... refused to disperse [and] hurled down stones in face of police firing".[31] By late 1930 or early 1931, a process of simultaneous decline and radicalization had set in: a weakening in forms of struggle associated with business groups or peasant upper strata (e.g. urban boycott, which merchants had started thinking involved too much of a financial sacrifice, or no-revenue in face of relentless British confiscation of property); accompanied by sporadic but fairly, widespread tendencies towards less manageable forms (e.g. popular violence, no-rent, tribal outbursts). It was in this situation, as I have argued elsewhere, that pressures for a compromise mounted and led on to the Gandhi-Irwin Pact.[32]

In August 1942, the bulk of the Congress leadership, and particularly Gandhi, were in an unusually militant mood, probably in large part because they felt that Britain was losing the war.[33] Yet despite strenuous efforts, the British failed to establish their case that the Congress before 9 August had really planned violent rebellion. Even the rather extreme secret circular of the Andhra PCC on 29 July 1942 had urged Congressmen to "be ready, organize at once, be alert, but by no means act... till Mahatmaji decides". It still emphasized in the main the traditional Gandhian forms, with no-tax as "practically the last stage", and mentioned disruption of communications (e.g. stopping trains "by pulling chains only") as "not prohibited but not encouraged".[34] This was still a far cry from the massive and violent attack on communications and all symbols of state authority which occurred in many parts of India after 9 August—what Linlithgow privately described as "by far the most serious rebellion since that of 1857, the gravity and extent of which we have so far concealed from the world for reasons of military security".[35] Once again, the principal catalysts, apart from war privations aggravated by ham-handed administrative measures like wholesale destruction of boats in Bengal, were the removal of Congress leaders (on the January 1932 pre-emptive strike model, but going far beyond it) and widespread hopes of imminent British collapse. This time, these were no longer vague rumours, but the undisputed fact of the ignominious British collapse in Malaya and Burma, with evacuees left in the lurch by the British flight and trainloads of wounded soldiers helping to spread the mood of anger and hostility towards what to most Indians was an alien and meaningless war, and expectation of an apocalyptic end to white rule.

Unlike in 1919-22 and 1930-34, the radicalization process in 1942 was on the whole mainly at the level of anti-British militancy alone, with the very extent of anti-foreign sentiments, as in 1857, possibly reducing internal class tensions and social radicalism. "The characteristic feature of this movement was that private property was not attacked," recalls the 1942 activist Govind Sahai,[36] and the socialist illegal pamphlet *Freedom Struggle Front* rather apologetically argued that "the class war may have to come, but that is not yet, not till after the riddance of foreign exploitation".[37] Though British authority virtually disappeared for some weeks over large parts of eastern UP and north Bihar, "there was only one attack on private property" in Azamgarh district,[38] (the estate of an absentee white zamindar), and, despite a strong and recent Kisan Sabha tradition in that area, Darbhanga raj officials noted with relief that rent-collection had remained unaffected.[39] Middle class nationalist ideology and organization may or may not have been indispensable in helping Indian peasants "to stand on their feet"; that it could also at times inhibit the articulation of class demands should not come as a surprise to anyone working within a Marxian framework.

Through a detailed comparative study of Agra, Rae Bareli, the Doab *tahsils* of Allahabad, and Bara Banki districts during Civil Disobedience, Gyan Pandey has established an important dualism about the role of Gandhian Congress organization.[40] Organizational strength and discipline undoubtedly made particular movements more effective, but it also inhibited elemental popular radicalism which was on the whole more evident in Non-Cooperation than in Civil Disobedience, for then Gandhi's message had had a stronger component of apocalyptic novelty. The same point emerges from a comparison over provinces: regions like rural CP, Maharashtra or Karnataka, where Non-Cooperation had been relatively weak and Gandhian penetration was still rather new in 1930, tended to have more uninhibited movements during Civil Disobedience, than already-established Congress bases like Gujarat, coastal Andhra or Bihar. As compared to UP, the Bengal Congress in the early 1930s was organizationally weak and remarkably faction-ridden; the Civil Disobedience era in that province combined less organized striking power with considerably greater diversity of forms of popular initiative.[41] In 1921-22, also, the most elemental and militant movements in Bengal were in relatively outlying parts of the province where Congress organizational penetration could not have gone very deep: the Jhargram sub-division of Midnapur, Rangpur, Chittagong hill regions (where reserved forests were invaded on a large scale), and Tippera.[42]

The Gandhian 'brakes' operated most obviously in the sudden halts which the leader imposed on the movements, as in the much-discussed retreats of February 1922 and March 1931.[43] But equally significant perhaps was the choice of issues for agitation by the Gandhian leadership, its very revealing 'silences': salt, no-revenue, non-*chaukidari* tax, but seldom no-rent; forest restrictions imposed by the colonial state, not many other tribal grievances; the opposition, except in August 1942, to political strikes.[44] Yet it is obvious that there was nothing *per se* 'violent' about no-rent or labour strikes; these could turn violent, but so could eminently acceptable forms like picketing of foreign goods.

It may be argued, with some justice, that any leadership, even an avowedly revolutionary one, has a necessarily restrictive aspect. It has to control spontaneity and sectional outbursts in the interests of long-term objectives and discipline. One may recall the role of Lenin and Trotsky in July 1917, or the Bolshevik suppression of the Kronstadt rising in 1921. It does not make much sense either to demand of Gandhi a social revolutionary perspective, and to condemn him for not behaving like Mao or Ho Chi-minh. But the argument often used to justify the Gandhian brakes and retreats—that these were necessary in the interests of overall anti-imperialist unity—fails to be entirely convincing once we raise the question as to the extent to which such methods were able in the end to realize the specific goals which Gandhian nationalism had set itself. That the Bardoli withdrawal caused a major setback was amply proved by the decline in nationalist tempo in the mid-1920s, marked by a disastrous slump in Congress membership (to 106,046 for 16 out of 20 provinces in March 1923, whereas UP alone had claimed 328,966 members in July 1921),[45] internal quarrels and rapid growth of both Hindu and Muslim communalism. The plea, put forward later on by Nehru, that the movement in early 1922 was going to pieces anyway, makes very odd reading if compared to contemporary official estimates. The secret history compiled by the Bengal government, for instance, emphasized that by the first quarter of 1922 "the movement had got beyond the control of the leaders... The spirit of violence and contempt of all authority which now began to show its head, was not of the leaders, but of masses".[46] This would appear to be a confirmation of much of R.P. Dutt's interpretation. Similar reservations apply to the Gandhi-Irwin Pact. The concessions offered at the first Round Table Conference, and the very fact of Irwin meeting Gandhi on terms of equality, revealed that the movement was far from defeated. It is true that the consequences of the Truce were much more ambiguous than those of the unilateral Bardoli withdrawal, for the Delhi Agreement did enhance Congress prestige and infuriated many bureaucrats. Yet the studies by Pandey of UP, Hardiman of Gujarat, and Stoddart of Andhra all agree that the Truce had very adverse consequences so far as the Congress political base among the peasantry was concerned: "The Gandhi Irwin pact broke the spirit of the Patidar peasants far more effectively than the lathis of the police".[47]

At a more general level, it is difficult to avoid the conclusion that Gandhian restraints inhibited the process of mobilization for the anti-imperialist cause of large sections of the poorer peasantry, tribals, and industrial workers. The Congress 'umbrella' was clearly tilted in favour of more propertied sections, for after all it was not always possible to please landlords and tenants, capitalists and workers, at the same time. Gandhian Congress mobilization, perhaps, was not "imperfect" so far as 'middle class' urban and rural propertied interests were concerned, for a broader range might well have proved socially dangerous; but it did limit the potential strength of the anti-imperialist movement—a much broader concept, it needs to be emphasized, than bourgeois nationalism. The consequences, in terms of the alienation of the Muslim peasantry of East Bengal, for instance, were too obvious to require much explication here. And if in the end India did win freedom basically under Gandhi's leadership, it must not be forgotten that this freedom left the Mahatma himself the most perplexed, isolated, and unhappy of men: for an yawning chasm separated his ideals of *ahimsa*, communal amity, Harijan upliftment, and peasant *ram-rajya* from the realities of 1947 and of post-independence India in general.

The Gandhian self-imposed limitations inevitably left a considerable variety of movements outside the ambit of mainstream nationalism. These may be classified into three broad types.

There were in the first place movements broadly continuing the patterns of pre-Gandhian spontaneous popular unrest directed against immediate oppressors, affected by Gandhi, if at all, only through distant rumours and not through any organizational linkages, and without much in the way of a leadership with all-India awareness or perspective. Food riots in the form of looting of village or small town *hats* remained an endemic, elementary form of popular reaction to sharp price-rise or excessive differentials between non-agricultural and agricultural prices. In Bengal, for instance, *hat* looting became particularly common during the 1918-19 price rise, and again in the Depression year of 1931 when agricultural prices fell much more sharply than those of industrial goods.[48] Widespread *hat* looting preceded the August 1942 upheaval in parts of North Bihar, and the sharp wartime rise in prices probably had something to do with the 92 dacoities reported from Bihar in April 1941, which represented a 100% rise over the average for the preceding three years.[49] Food riots could occasionally coincide with broader movements without becoming intrinsically a part of them. In January 1921, there were 35 cases of *hat* looting in the North Bihar districts of Muzaffarpur, Bhagalpur, Monghyr and Purnea, with men who claimed to be Gandhi's disciples trying to enforce just prices.[50] The Kisan Sabha movement in Awadh led in the same month to agrarian riots attacking both *talukdars* and *banias,* and Fursatganj bazaar in Rae Bareli district was attacked on 6 January by a crowd of 6000 demanding that "all the shopkeepers should at once be ordered to sell cloth at 4 annas per yard and flour at 8 seers per rupee".[51] But *hat* looting could form part of communal riots, too, where traders and rural consumers belonged to different religious groups— as happened, for instance, in the riots in and around Dacca in May 1930.[52]

Among tribal movements during the inter-war years, that led by Alluri Sitarama Raju in the 'Rampa' region between August 1922 and May 1924 deserves special attention for its transitional, intermediate position between 'primitive rebellion' and modern nationalism. Developing in the wake of a Congress-inspired forest *satyagraha* in neighbouring Guntur district, it was led by an outsider who had wandered among the tribals from 1915 claiming astrological and healing powers and had been marginally connected with Non-Cooperation activities. Sitarama Raju in a meeting with local officials during the rebellion "spoke , highly of Mr. Gandhi", but considered "that violence is necessary".[53] The tribals under his leadership showed remarkable discrimination between whites and Indians, allowing (at the Damarapalli ambush of 24 September 1922) an advance party of Indians to pass before shooting down the two British officers.[54] Yet the grievances were very similar to those which had already inspired so many rebellions in the same region—moneylender exploitation, forest restrictions, use of unpaid tribal labour by officials—and Raju claimed that he was bullet-proof, and issued a proclamation announcing the imminent coming of *Kalki-Avatar*.[55] The combination produced an extremely effective guerrilla struggle, with a stable band of about a hundred, and "supernumeraries all over the disturbed area who joined it whenever it was in their locality"[56] —in other words, fish in water enjoying widespread popular support. It required the Malabar Special Police and the Assam Rifles nearly two years and Rs. 15 lakhs to suppress this guerrilla struggle.[57]

Despite a new awareness of tribal problems reflected in Congress-organized forest *satyagrahas*, some Gandhian welfare activities, and certain links established with groups like the Tana Bhagats and Sapha Hors,[58] the majority of tribal movements remained outside the ambit of mainstream nationalism. Congress interest even in forest grievances was limited and intermittent. There is no evidence of any nationalist involvement, for instance, in the forest movements of the Saoras in Ganjam agency in 1927 and during 1937-40, or in the Gond rising against forest restrictions in Adilabad district of Hyderabad state in 1940,[59] With the development of a tribal educated middle class elite, the ground was prepared also for increasingly 'sectional' or 'separatist' tribal movements, particularly in the North-East and in Chotanagpur. These received considerable encouragement at times from missionaries, certain British officials, and some anthropologists, but, as in the not dissimilar cases of Muslim communal and Scheduled Caste movements, 'divide and rule' was greatly helped by Congress inhibitions about socially explosive issues.

The autonomous and powerful anti-landlord Kisan movements of the early 1920s, of which the Darbhanga Raj agitation under Swami Vidyanand in 1919-20 and the Awadh awakening under Baba Ramchandra in 1920-21 are the best-known,[60] also have a transitional character. Despite occasional militant outbursts and participation by the rural poor,[60a] these seem to have been essentially movements of the upper stratum of the tenantry, predominantly Bhumihar

Brahman in Bihar and Kurmis and other intermediate castes in UP, with fairly, limited objectives (an end to *amla* extortion and threats to occupancy rights in the Darbhanga Raj; reduction in cesses and *begar* and resistance to *bedakhli* or eviction in Awadh). The Kisan Sabhas of the 1930s would also fight often for limited aims, but the essential difference would be the existence by then of an overall perspective of social transformation, brought by outsider intellectuals with a more or less socialist ideology, and crystallized in the demand for abolition of zamindari within a clear anti-imperialist framework. Baba Ramchandra in contrast began by urging "union between *zamindar, kisan* and *majdoor*", though he later became bitterly disillusioned about Congress hesitation in espousing peasant causes and developed an admiration for Lenin and Russia.[61] Swami Vidyanand got diverted to electoral politics in late 1920,[62] and, through Malaviya's protege Indra Narain Dwivedi, the UP liberals were able to retain a connection with a minority section of the kisan movement in that province. The majority, including Baba Ramchandra, passed under Congress control through the efforts of Jawaharlal and Gaurishankar Misra, but found its specific anti-talukdar demands largely swallowed up by Non-Cooperation.[63] It is important to note that *kisan* movements with class demands seem to have flourished mainly in periods marked by a relative ebb-tide in nationalist agitation. Thus the Bihar Kisan Sabha, though formally founded in 1929, really got into its stride under Swami Sahajanand after the collapse of Civil Disobedience, from about 1934 onwards.[64] In Bengal, too, there were interesting tenant and sharecropper movements in the mid-1920s which virtually disappeared in 1930, were resumed to some extent in the Truce period, and gathered strength from the mid-1930s.[65]

With Kisan Sabhas and trade unions under Left leadership and Communist and CSP political activities among toilers, we enter a somewhat different world: a second brand of non-Gandhian popular movements, characterized by a conscious, alternative and more radical type of anti-imperialism integrally bound up with a vision of socio-economic change. Though Comintern ideological influence and organizational assistance did have a certain role here, the main impetus came from within the national movement itself, as elements disillusioned by Gandhian compromises (or, particularly in Bengal, by the heroic blind alley of revolutionary terrorism) sought new roads to freedom and social transformation. The initial breakthrough was on the industrial labour front which unfortunately has so far attracted much less detailed or sophisticated research than the history of peasant movements. Labour history in our country, as well as the history of the Left political movements in general, tends to get reduced to a catalogue of strikes and unions, to collections of reminiscences about top leaders, or to endless and often rather sterile ideological controversies concerning the correctness or otherwise of a particular political 'line'. A 'history from below' in this largely unexplored field would probably lead to a greater emphasis on the forms of consciousness and self-activity of the working class, without belittling of course the indispensable and often heroic role of pioneer labour organizers. The initiative for the massive post-War labour upsurge came mainly from below, for in the early 1920s most trade unions were very far from being believers in unlimited class war. The general strike in Bombay textiles of January 1919, for instance, was basically spontaneous, and labour rallies repeatedly rejected the counsels of moderation offered by Home Rule League politicians like Kanji Dwarkadas and Umar Sobhani.[66] The Jamshedpur Labour Association founded by S.N. Halder and Byomkesh Chakrabarti in course of the February 1920 Tata strike could provide only very compromising and inept guidance,[67] and Subhas Bose's intervention in 1928 was little better. After a conversation with him, G.D. Birla reported to Purshottamdas Thakurdas on 16 July 1929 that "I feel in a position to assure that Mr. Bose could be relied upon to help the Tata Iron and Steel Works whenever necessary provided properly handled".[68]

The Communist entry into the Bombay and Calcutta industrial area on a large scale in 1928-29 signified a qualitatively new stage, displacing to a considerable extent the jobbers whom previous trade union leaders had perforce used as intermediaries and encouraging within the Gimi Kamgar Union an element of grassroots democratization through a structure of elected mill committees.[69] The private correspondence of Governor Sykes of Bombay and Governor Stanley Jackson of Bengal vividly reflects the holy fear inspired among British rulers by this combination of labour militancy and revolutionary ideology,[70] and a *Yugantar* terrorist who later became a communist leader has recalled how the sight of Lilluah workers on march flanked by armed police inspired in him the first vision of an alternative and more effective path to revolution.[71] Despite the marked inhibitions of the nationalist leadership, workers' participation in anti-imperialist actions, was by no means negligible at times. One may cite as stray examples the prominence of jute mill hands among volunteers courting arrest in Calcutta during the last phase of the Non-Cooperation-Khilafat upsurge,[71a] the massive labour march to the Calcutta Congress in December 1928 demanding *Purna Swaraj*, and the widespread strikes in the early days of the Quit India movement, when the Tata Steel Plant, for instance, was closed down for thirteen days in a strike in which the sole labour slogan was that workers "will not resume work until a national government has been formed".[71b]

By the late 1930s, the Left had built up a number of country-wide organizations of trade unions, *kisan sabhas*, students, and intellectuals, and exercised a certain influence on the top nationalist leadership as a major pressure group within the Congress as well as through personal contacts and affinities with Nehru and Bose, but could still be outgeneralled, as Tripuri and its sequel proved, by the Congress Right and Gandhi. The Left, however, did not yet really have the capacity to launch effective all-India political struggles on its own. 1942 broke up the always uneasy but still crucial alliance between Communists and Congress Socialists which had been the core of the pre-War Left alternative, and rehabilitated the prestige of Rightist Congress leaders who had been in serious danger of losing credibility among the masses during the period of Congress ministries.[72] Yet the strike wave of 1946 far surpassed all previous records: 1629 stoppages, involving 1,941,948 workers and the loss of 12,717,762 man-days. In no previous year had strikes exceeded 1,000 or the workers involved 8 lakhs.[73] As revealed by the massive explosions in Calcutta on 21-23 November 1945 and 11-13 February 1946 on the INA trials issue, followed by the upsurge in Bombay during the RIN revolt, workers and urban masses in general were increasingly coming out into the streets on political issues. When taken in conjunction with the Tebhaga movement in the winter of 1946-47, the beginning of the Telengana armed struggle in July 1946, the Punnapra-Vayalar uprising in October 1946, and militant movements for democratization and integration in many princely states, we are left with the impression of something like a countrywide upsurge. And for the first time since the rise of Gandhi, this was an upsurge that was not only independent of the Mahatma and the entire Congress leadership, but taking place against their repeated and explicit directives.[74]

Yet the tragic paradox was that the same years saw unprecedented communal riots—Calcutta, Noakhali, Bihar, Punjab—which directly led up to the Partition. Communalism in both its 'elite' and 'mass' manifestations had kept pace with the development of mass nationalism. Its growth was particularly evident in the mid-1920s after the collapse of Non-Cooperation and Khilafat, under the Congress ministries of 1937-39 when for the first time the

Muslim League attempted to develop into a mass party, and during the War when the League (and to some extent the Hindu Mahasabha) took advantage of the suppression of the Congress. With some exceptions (like the Satyashodhak movement in Maharashtra, brought under the nationalist wing in the 1930s through a new non-Brahman Congress provincial leadership),[75] the Congress also failed to win over political organizations of lower castes, notably Ambedkar's Mahar-based movement, or the elite Justice and more populist Self-Respect traditions in Tamilnad, despite Gandhi's increasing insistence on Harijan welfare work. Political devolution (which, the British insisted had to be by stages and through separate representation), increasing competition for jobs as spread of education coincides with shrinking of opportunities, and differential bourgeois growth all stimulated elite conflicts, and the Congress was not able in practice to implement programmes, sufficiently and consistently secular and radical, with which to undercut links along religious or caste lines between such elites and their clientele. The Gandhian Congress itself in fact at times tried to utilize and work through such vertical linkages: as during the Khilafat alliance with the *ulema*, the continued alignment with the socially obscurantist but anti-League Deoband group, or Gandhi's close relations with Madanmohan Malaviya in the 1920s. Things changed somewhat in the late-1930s under the influence of Nehru and the Congress Left, but Muslim "mass contact" still remained largely on paper. Secular and radical rhetoric, seldom backed up by concrete measures, in the end merely alarmed Muslim vested interests without winning over the Muslim masses. Social inhibitions apart, there was the further basic fact of continual interpenetration, at both elite and mass levels, of forms of consciousness—national, regional, caste, communal, class—theoretically distinct but in practice at times almost impossible to disentangle. Thus, despite the adoption of numerous unimpeachable secular resolutions in the 1930s,

Azad had to complain in 1937 that Congressmen in the Central Provinces could not join the League, but were often to be found active in the Hindu Mahasabha.[76] In much of northern and central India, in fact, Congress-led rural populism was often deeply intermingled with Hinduism and the use of Hindi in tacit or open opposition to relatively more urbanized Muslims and upper-class Urdu culture. Baba Ramchandra, to take a second example; combined appeals for *kisan* solidarity with considerable use of a religious idiom and caste slogans, choosing Roor as base for the first Kisan Sabha possibly because of an alleged reference to it in Tulsidas, and being active also in a Kurmi Kshatriya Sabha.[77] Swami Sahajanand, too began as a Bhumihar Brahman reformer and organizer, though he went far beyond it. Even the Left, one has to admit, has on the whole failed to confront the problems of caste oppression and religious bigotry with sufficient seriousness,[78] with the result that economic or political militancy among workers or *kisans* has seldom been accompanied by any significant transformation in their cultural horizons. Kerala possibly represents a partial exception, for there the "advantages of backwardness" in the shape of particularly atrocious caste barriers and a late start in social reforms as compared to regions like Bengal made passage from such reform to radical politics remarkably uninterrupted.[79]

As in the section dealing with the pre-Gandhian phase, it may be appropriate at this stage to formulate some tentative generalizations about the impact of popular initiatives, both inside and outside the Gandhian mainstream. Gyan Pandey has rightly argued that

> ...the belligerent UP peasant of the early 1930s advanced the nationalist movement by one significant step. It was his struggle that made the Congress leadership aware at last, though by no means fully, of the gravity and significance of the peasant question and led them to relate it to the concept of *swaraj*, making it somewhat more lucid and concrete than ever before.[80]

The shift in Congress attitudes epitomized by the Faizpur agrarian programme, the tenancy legislations in Congress-ruled states in 1937-39, and the eventual abolition of zamindaries after independence are all clearly related to the pressure of peasant movements. The emergence of organized labour in the 1920s similarly led to the incorporation of some worker demands in Congress manifestoes from the Karachi statement on fundamental rights onwards, and the quite remarkable change in the style and language of Congress programmatic declarations by the late 1930s as compared to earlier decades, their increasing use of a socialistic idiom; was certainly not due to the personal influence, however significant, of Jawaharlal Nehru alone. Congress policy towards princely states also underwent a major revision, again under the pressure of a multitude of more or less radical states people's movements. In the second place, specific popular pressures did lead at times to official concessions: good examples would be the Oudh Rent Act of 1921 in the wake of Baba Ramchandra's movement, and the tacit abandonment of revenue enhancements following the Bardoli experience of 1928. At a more general level, it was the extension through popular pressures of Non-Cooperation, Civil Disobedience, and Quit India alike that really forced significant policy changes on the British. By late 1921, the sweep of Non-Cooperation and Khilafat, going far beyond programmes sanctioned by the leadership, forced Reading in secret telegrams to Montagu to suggest release of prisoners, a Round Table Conference, and an early revision of the newly-implemented Reform scheme[81]—anticipations of the 1930s which came to nothing because of Gandhi's unilateral withdrawal after Chauri Chaura. Though Irwin had complacently assured Wedgewood Benn on 20 February 1930 that "the prospect of a salt campaign does not keep me awake at night",[82] Civil Disobedience proved dangerous enough to lead to a swift abandonment of the Simon Report, the formal acceptance of responsible government in the centre at the first session of the Round Table Conference, and the opening of negotiations with Gandhi on a novel basis of equality. The August 1942 impact proved even more decisive: the British would never again risk such a confrontation, and the decision of the Labour Government to try for a negotiated settlement with the Congress (already anticipated in fact by the no means ultra-liberal Wavell[83]) stands in very sharp contrast to the deliberately provocative policies that had led to the torpedoing of the Cripps initiative and to the Quit India movement itself.

I have argued elsewhere[84] that popular pressures in 1945-47 played an extremely important role in determining the course of events that led upto the coming of freedom with Partition—a fact somewhat obscured by the tendency among historians so far to study top level negotiations in isolation. The three decisive shifts in British policy—the tacit abandonment of INA trials and the Cabinet Mission announcement in the winter of 1945-46, the decision to allow Nehru to form a purely Congress Interim Government in September 1946, and Attlee's speech of 20 February 1947 fixing a deadline for transfer of power—can all be related fairly directly to such pressures. Fear of popular 'excesses' and social upheaval, again, made Congress leaders cling to the path of negotiation and compromise, and eventually accept even Partition as the necessary price. A week after the Calcutta upsurge of 21-23 November 1945, New Delhi informed London that the INA trials policy would have to be modified, since "abstract justice must to some extent give way to expediency".[85] Wavell recognized the Calcutta disturbances as a "turning point" in Congress leadership attitudes, causing "at least a temporary detente".[86] G.D. Birla on 6 December assured a London official: "There is no political leader including Jawaharlal who wants to see any crisis or violence... Popular impatience and the prevalent atmosphere are responsible for these strong speeches. Even leaders are often led. But I think unrestrained language will be heard less and less in the future".[87] Congress and League leaders showed rare unanimity in opposing the RIN mutiny and the sympathetic general strike in Bombay, and the provincial bosses of the two parties (S.K. Patil and Chundrigar) even "offered the help of volunteers to assist the police".[88] On 5 August 1946, to take a second example, Wavell received information that Patil was prepared to threaten resignation if the Working Committee rejected his plea that "the Congress must enter the Government to prevent chaos spreading in the country"[89]—this was, it must be noted, *before* the Calcutta communal holocaust. The Director of the Intelligence made the underlying British logic crystal clear an 9 August:

> ...the labour situation is becoming increasingly dangerous... Until a responsible Indian government is introduced at the Centre, there is little that can be done. The Communists are only part of a larger nettle which must be grasped. I am satisfied that a responsible government, if one can be achieved, will deal more decisively with labour than is at present possible.[90]

A similar pattern was at work next year in the accession, followed in 1948 by integration, of princely states, managed in record time by Sardar Patel and V.P. Menon through a skilful combination of threats of mass pressure—for which the existence of powerful people's movements was indispensable—and baits of limited accession and generous offers of privy purses and offices of *Rajpramukhs*.

Thus pressures from below were the necessary catalysts of decisive changes, and yet popular forces were largely denied the fruits of victory, since political independence was successfully detached from radical socio-economic change through a 'peaceful' transfer of power which also proved to be an unimaginably bloody communal holocaust and a tragic Partition. A history from below cannot avoid the problem of exploration of the roots of this ultimate failure.

At a somewhat superficial but not irrelevant level, the explanation can be offered in terms of superior leadership skills. The Congress leadership under Gandhi combined a rare ability to choose specific and very concrete and evocative issues and forms of agitation; with an awareness of the importance of limited but real gains through constructive work among the rural masses,[91] and a capacity for the right gestures and accommodations, offering openings to the Left repeatedly at programmatic levels while seldom conceding the substance. The result was a very successful process, in Gramscian terms, of *transformismo,* bringing about "the gradual but continuous absorption.... of the active elements produced by allied groups—and even of those which came from antagonistic groups and seemed irreconcilably hostile".[92] The process was epitomized by the 'taming' of Nehru, thrust into the top leadership position by Gandhi in 1929 and again in 1936 in his most militant mood, given responsibility without decisive power is a predominantly conservative Working Committee,[93] and gradually transformed from the flaming radical of the 1930s to a man with whom Indian capitalists could work sometimes even more satisfactorily than with Gandhi himself, despite some socialist elements in his ideology which perhaps never entirely disappeared. The combination of populist and socialist rhetoric with much less radical practice would in fact become a major feature of the post-independence regime. It needs to be added that the British on their part also showed considerable flexibility, despite occasional bouts of bloody-minded obstinacy (as in 1919, Civil Disobedience, or 1939-42), offering concessions which were on the whole not too belated. A more rigid stance could certainly have pushed the bulk of the nationalist movement towards more militant strategies. And while Lancashire long remained pig-headed about its vanishing captive market, the private papers of Edward Benthall, the boss of Bird Company, reveal certain other sections of British business skilfully developing an accommodation with their Indian counterparts.[94]

The popular pressures, in contrast, often tended to remain scattered potentially radical outbursts rather than develop into a coherent national alternative. The organized Left, typified above all in the Communist movement, never really solved the crucial problem which plagued it throughout, from the Second Comintern Congress of 1920—that of its relationship with the bourgeois-led nationalist mainstream. It tended to swing wildly and repeatedly between 'sectarian' and 'reformist' poles, an oscillation which a Comintern dominated by Stalin and Soviet foreign policy interests did little to prevent and much to encourage. The combination of broad multi-class objectives with retention of initiative and independence was seldom achieved here—in sharp contrast to the Chinese experience under Mao in the anti-Japanese war, or (a lesser-known but interesting, example) the Bolsheviks themselves, who retained upto the very eve of October 1917 a very modest 'bourgeois-democratic' minimum programme, but certainly never expected bourgeois parties like the Kadets to carry out this programme for them. In colonial India, too, substantial advances were made in regions like Kerala or Telengana by communists taking over the initiative and leadership in the national struggle, as when P. Krishna Pillai, E.M.S. Namboodiripad and A.K. Gopalan during the 1930s simultaneously built up the Congress, the CSP as legal cover, and the illegal CPI in Travancore and Malabar. But all too often united front came to mean a policy of waiting on bourgeois leaders and putting undeserved trust in their 'progressive' declarations—an attitude which in its turn repeatedly bred an equally disastrous relapse into ultra-left sectarianism.

Yet leadership successes and failures can provide only a small part of the answer. We need to consider at this point also the broad social composition and nature of the movements led by Gandhi and their radical would-be alternatives. It is in terms of this social composition that we must ultimately explain the basic fact that the participants in Gandhian movements on the whole accepted the brakes imposed by the leader without major disillusionment.

As in the pre-Gandhian phase, a major part of the nationalist activists came from the urban or small town 'middle class' intelligentsia with considerable links with petty rentier interests, and much of the inhibition shown on agrarian questions by the national leadership can be related to this important social fact. A new element under Gandhi was the growing participation by specifically bourgeois groups, which the Thakurdas papers and other business collections now allow us to document with some precision. An important consequence was a marked hesitation to involve workers overmuch in the national struggle. It was probably not a coincidence that both Non-Cooperation and Civil Disobedience were launched after, and not during, peak points of labour unrest. Political strikes were sanctioned by the Gandhian leadership in August 1942—at a time, one might argue, when their radicalization was less likely due to the Communist attitude. Gandhi showed little sympathy for the strike wave of 1945-47,[95] and in general the working class was the one significant element in Indian society to remain largely unaffected by Gandhian ideology, except for the rather special case of Ahmedabad. The growth of the INTUC was a very late and largely post-independence phenomenon. More generally, business support for national movements was always limited by the constant fear of radical 'excesses', and bourgeois pressures for compromise settlements or greater moderation seem fairly well-documented, particularly for the Gandhi-Irwin Pact, the formation and policies of the Congress ministries in 1937-39, and the 1945-47 period.[96] Such fears have been a recurrent element in bourgeois behaviour in many other countries and times, and can be explained in terms of a fairly rational calculation of class interest. But Indian business groups fell short of the 'national bourgeois' stereotype also in their frequent preference for sectional over country-wide class interests: as when Birla patronized the Hindu Mahasabha and Malaviya against the Swarajists in the 1920s, or Muslim businessmen like Adamjee or Ispahani provided much of the sinews of war for the Pakistan movement. The assumptions that the Indian capitalist class "revealed a basic homogeneity in its economic and political relationship with imperialism"[96a] and that G.D. Birla can be taken to have been its typical representative in the 1930s and 40s, appear to involve a considerable over-simplification. The Tatas combined greater involvement with really modern industrialization and loyalism; Bombay mill owners often opposed the Congress, and South Indian capitalist groups also had little connection with the national movement till the formation of the Congress ministry in Madras.

The specific nature of the Gandhian rural base is a much more formidable problem. Categorization of the kind of peasant strata which responded most to Gandhi is rendered difficult both by great regional variations, as well as by the well-known complexities of applying theoretical schema of peasant stratification to data which is incomplete and arranged according to quite different principles. The Bolsheviks faced enormous difficulties in the 1920s in their efforts to translate Lenin's distinctions between rich, middle and poor peasants into politically operational categories despite the accumulation of massive data and highly sophisticated methods of 'budget studies' and 'dynamic studies' of households.[97] The problems are probably even more intractable for pre-independence India. Thus, as Utsa Patnaik has pointed out in an important paper, class categories often cut right across tenancy categories (due to considerable leasing-out by small landholders), and even her own 'labour exploitation ratio' (i.e. the ratio of use of outside labour to family labour) fails to provide a fully satisfactory test for the capitalist rich peasant, due to the importance in Indian conditions of pre-capitalist employer-labourer relations based on caste and bonded labour.[98] Attempts to apply Hamza Alavi's 'middle peasant' thesis have also run into difficulties connected with the problem of distinguishing between the 'rich' and the 'middle' strata as revealed for instance, by Hardiman's uncertainties in characterizing the Kheda *patidars*.[99] Regional variations add to the complexities. Thus D.A. Low's 'dominant peasant' argument[100] fits the *patidars* fairly well, but it is difficult to apply to Arambagh.[101] Rural prosperity also seems at times to have weakened the nationalist appeal—the peasant response to 1942 was relatively weak in Gujarat,[102] almost non-existent in the Punjab with its extra income from military service, and, less evident in western than in eastern UP.

One may still hazard a few very tentative generalizations, relevant for our basic problem of explaining the effectiveness of Gandhian constraints. Gandhian peasant movements do seem to have been most effective where the rural scene was not too sharply polarized, and where there existed a fairly broad stratum of small holders preferably more or less homogeneous in caste composition: good examples would be the *patidars* of Kheda of Bardoli, the *mahishyas* of Tamluk and Contai the Jat peasantry of districts like Meerut during Civil Disobedience, or, as Washbrook has argued, the coastal Andhra region as contrasted to the 'dry' districts of interior Tamil Nadu where a less favourable ecology sharpened rural differences.[103]

In the second place, while Gandhian bases were occasionally established in very backward pockets like Arambagh (where the extent of isolation and poverty could make the marginal improvements brought about through devoted constructive work all the more politically effective), most of the strongholds tended to be in regions marked not by maximum impoverishment, but by a threat to relative prosperity or social and economic advance. This, applies not only to districts like Kheda, where a period of *patidar* upthrust was cut short by famine, plague, and price fluctuations in the early twentieth century,[104] but also perhaps to Rae Bareli, a district characterized in the 1920s by a combination of rapidly-increasing double cropping, considerable well-irrigation and improvements in communications, a consequent spurt in grain, poppy and oilseeds exports, along with absence of occupancy rights and prevalence of *bedakhli* and *nazrana* by big *talukdars* which obviously threatened the incipient relative prosperity of Kurmi or Ahir cultivators.[105] In Pratapgarh, too, the soil was fertile, irrigated land comprised 58% of the total cultivated area already by 1896, and the Kurmis (an "excellent class of cultivators" according to a Settlement Report) were building fine wells, which the *talukdars*, however, used as an excuse to impose additional *nazrana*.[106] Although... "three-fifths of the district were held by fairly substantial tenants in holdings of 5 or more acres" rents were exceptionally high and rapidly increasing.[107]

It may be argued, finally, that irrespective of the precise social composition of the movement in a particular area, the general thrust, ideology and style of Gandhian nationalism was geared objectively to the interests of landholding intermediate-caste peasant proprietors or tenants, and not to the subordinate stratum of tribal or low-caste agricultural labourers, sharecroppers, and poorest peasants. Harijan upliftment, however sincere, was confined in the main to humanitarian work and symbolic concessions like temple entry or use of wells. The aim was a certain humanizing of existing structures of caste and class hierarchies in the countryside, not their overthrow. Even this was often severely restricted by the hostility of dominant village groups who were in every other respect Gandhi's most loyal followers—as when Narhari Parikh's move to start a school among Dubla semi-tribal bonded labour in Bardoli was blocked by fierce *patidar* opposition. When Parikh threatened a protest fast, "the Patidars told him that they did not care if he died."[108] During the Bardoli *satyagraha* of 1928, extensive use was made of the existing caste organizations, and Patel's speeches and the *Satyagraha Patrika* repeatedly stressed traditional ties of dependence of Dublas and artisans on *patidar* peasant landholders, as well as those between peasants and Vania trader-moneylenders.[109] The combination of 'patronage' and 'exploitation' which Jan Breman has found in another part of Surat in Anavil Brahman-Dubla relationships come in very useful here.[110] Ghanshyam Shah in his analysis of eight speeches made by Patel during the 1928 *satyagraha* records 34 references to faith in God and 27 to loyalty to community or caste.[111] Thus traditional religious and caste sentiments were at best subsumed, and never dissolved, in the nationalist tide—to reappear often with a vengeance later on, as the vicious anti-Harijan riots in Gandhi's own Gujarat has recently revealed.

For the peasant upper crust with something to lose in terms of both caste and class privilege, the Gandhian strategy of mass participation controlled and limited by *ahimsa* had a natural appeal, for more uninhibited movements could well prove dangerous—as Kheda peasants were forcibly reminded of, when Baraiyas inspired by rumours of breakdown of British authority in the wake of the 1918 *satyagraha* started looting rich Charotar villages.[112] There was thus an objective basis for the alliance between urban bourgeois groups and the peasant upper stratum around the Gandhian programme of controlled mass action. An alliance not without its tensions, however: Indian folk tales, after all, are replete with images of *bania* traders-cum-moneylenders as villainous oppressors of the peasantry, and the Gandhi-Irwin Pact seems to have been a definite case of sacrifice of peasant interests to business pressures for a truce. One may note in passing that the apparent radicalization of Gandhi in his last years was possibly connected with a certain detachment of the Mahatma from urban capitalist groups —which increasingly found Nehru with his vision of modernist industrialization more congenial, once it was realized that his socialism could definitely be 'tamed'—and a corresponding shift to a more extreme rural populism. "If mills flourish *khadi* must die", declared Gandhi in a *Harijan* article of 20 October 1946,[113] denouncing Congress ministerial patronage to the Indian textile industry, and he also pressed for decontrol of food in the last weeks of his life, on the grounds that rationing and state procurement meant corruption and feeding the towns at the expense of the villages.[114] Gandhi's last days have a grandeur all their own, springing not only from the heroic fight against communalism ending in martyrdom, but also from his repeated attacks on Congress corruption, bureaucracy and greed for power; culminating in the startling proposal of 29 January 1948 to dissolve the Congress as a political party.[115] Yet it remains important to remember that the basic hostility to revolutionary change in property relations was never discarded in April 1947, Gandhi had warned that neglect of constructive work could lead to "rivers of blood and a holocaust such as you cannot today envisage... the tide of Communism would overwhelm them".[116] The alternative posed by him points towards Jayaprakash Narayan and the more or less reactionary Janata brand of rich peasant-based populism, rather than any coherent perspective for the emancipation of toilers of town or countryside.

The Leftists, of course, did not share Gandhi's inhibitions about class war. But the peasant movements led by them could not entirely escape the ambiguities imposed by regional differences, very complex agrarian relations, and, above all, the unusually sharp caste-rooted distinction between landholding peasants and the landless characteristic of the Indian rural scene. The Kisan Sabhas of the 1930s and early 40s with their anti-big zamindar thrust and focus on issues like reduction in revenue, canal rates and debt and remunerative prices were primarily organizations of peasants with some, at times considerable, land, and not of agricultural labourers. Sahajanand in a late 1936 issue of the *Kisan Bulletin* visualized improvement in conditions of landless labour "by negotiating with the peasants, and by assisting their organized strike against zamindars and planters"—an interesting, though not unnatural, distinction.[117] The Election Manifesto of the CPI in 1945 gave an assurance that the Party "shall not touch the small zamindar or the rich peasant but shall open before them the prospect of becoming the best of the farmers and cattle-breeders, reputed members in their own village".[118] Even the Telengana armed struggle was directed mainly against high-caste Hindu and Muslim big *deshmukhs* and *jagirdars,* and the ceiling the Communists sought to impose in the liberated areas for redistribution of land was fixed at a fairly high level of 100 acres dry and 10 acres wet.[119] It made perfectly good political sense for a long time to concentrate on all—in peasant unity against big landlords. But the problem was that partial gains like the abolition of zamindari and some limited redistribution through largely theoretical ceilings, carried out by post-1947 Congress governments mainly under pressure of peasant movements climaxed by Telengana, tended to make the peasant upper layer politically conservative fairly quickly—as happened on a large scale in coastal Andhra and Telengana itself during the 1950s.

The Communist tradition in India, particularly in its more militant phases or segments, also includes considerable work among tribals, sharecroppers, agricultural labourers and poor peasants: the Hajongs under Moni Singh in the late 1930s, the Worlis of Thana organized by Godavari Parulekar, the Tebhaga mobilization of Rajbansi sharecroppers, the last stand of the Telengana guerrillas in the predominantly tribal Godavari forests where Alluri Sitarama Raju had once fought, and—of course—Naxalbari and Srikakulam. The recurrent and as yet unsolved problem here has been the danger of isolation and alienation from the bulk of the peasantry, for a crucial feature of the Indian real scene is that the most oppressed sections, *adivasis* and *Harijans,* are a minority, and their oppressors include not only landlords and big farmers but also small peasants who tend often to be extra conscious of their superiority over castes still lower than them in the social and economic scale. As for labour, its concrete achievements in the building up of a fairly strong countrywide trade union movement should not be underestimated; if it has remained basically 'economistic' and confined to partial gains, so have most agrarian movements which nowadays it has become somewhat fashionable to romanticize. But politicization has certainly lagged far behind trade union militancy—even today, the centres of political influence of the communist parties do not have much relationship (outside Bengal) with an industrial map of the country. A few special cases like the Punnapra-Vayalar rising of October 1946 apart,[120] the worker-peasant (or rural proletariat) alliance has remained more a theoretical ideal than reality. And proletarianization, whether before or after independence, has certainly not solved automatically the problems of caste and communal fragmentation.

A fuller explication of the limits of popular movements requires also a study of cultural dimensions. The study of the popular, and particularly peasant mind has hardly begun as yet,[121] but a few tentative hints may be derived from extant studies of movements and from a very limited reading of folk-tale collections. The contradictory aspects of the function of rumour have already been mentioned, in particular the peasant tendency to look for a saviour from above, producing the phenomenon of what Rude has termed the "involuntary leader"[122]—such as Gandhi seems to have been for many during the years of his initial impact. A conviction that victory was near at hand, if not already achieved, seems also to have been necessary, at least for a real *levee en masse* of the countryside. In eastern UP and Bihar in August 1942, peasants marched in their thousands on police stations, fired with the belief that white rule had collapsed; often their aims were no more than symbolical, to replace the British with the national flag. When the British presence massively reasserted itself, such mobilization quickly gave way to passivity or at best some clandestine assistance to fairly small bands of freedom-fighters.

Folk-tales certainly do not convey an impression of a conflict-free or harmonious countryside, nor of an entirely passive world of the poor. But they are full of ambiguities—thus if there are some cults of social bandits, numerous stories also emphasize the duty of respecting upper castes, particularly Brahmans.[123] A very common theme is the defeat of the rich and powerful by the poor and weak, carried over often, as in other countries, to animal tales. But the poor man typically outmatches his oppressor not through any kind of joint action, but through an individual battle of wits, and often at great cost to himself. Thus Bhar Bitna, a dwarf with only one buffalo, manages to trick the rich Mahtaji with extensive lands repeatedly in a Bihari tale, and ends up living happily ever after having seized Mahtaji's land and wealth.[124] The Punjabi folk tale about the farmer and the moneylender is more pathetic, and perhaps more realistic. The moneylender stole the wish-fulfilling conch given to the poor farmer by Rama, but not knowing how to use it, struck a bargain with the peasant by which he would have double of whatever the former wished for. The peasant got out of the *bania's* clutches only by wishing to be blinded in one eye.[125] Oppressors and forms of oppression may have changed somewhat with the times, but not perhaps the underlying realities so vividly revealed in such tales.

NOTES

1. No doubt the loyalist Justice and Non-Brahman parties in Madras and Maharashtra were greatly stimulated by the possibility of special reservations, and even Jawaharlal's wanderings among the *kisans* were welcomed by his father, as late as June 1920, for improving the former's electoral chances. Siddiqi, *Agrarian Unrest*, p. 129.
2. G. Blyn, *Agricultural Trends in India 1891-1947: Output, Availability and Productivity* (Pennsylvania, 1966), Chapter V.
3. Stephen Henningham, *Protest and Control in North Bihar, India, 1917-1942: A Study of Conflict and Continuity in a Colonial*

Agrarian Society (unpublished Ph.D. Thesis, ANU, 1978, available in microfiche at the Nehru Museum, New Delhi), Chapter 1.

4. *Census of India, 1931, Volume XVIII (United Provinces)*, Part 1, p. 112.
5. David Hardiman, *Peasant Nationalists*, Chapter 9.
6. G. Lefebvre, "Revolutionary Crowds", reprinted in J. Kaplow (ed.), *New Perspectives on the French Revolution: Readings in Historical Sociology* (New York, 1965), p. 175.

6a. Judith Brown, *Gandhi's Rise to Power: Indian Politics, 1915-22* (Cambridge, 1972). A rather peculiar phrase, surely, for at the end of the "rise" Gandhi was in jail and his movement apparently shattered.

7. While even Tilak, Lajpat Rai or Bipin Pal had had essentially regional bases, the peculiar circumstances of South Africa had brought together Hindus, Muslims, Parsis, Christians, Gujaratis, South Indians, prosperous merchants and lawyers, and Newcastle mine workers in a common fight against gross racial discrimination under Gandhi's leadership. It is a remarkable fact that 13 out of the first 25 inmates of Sabarmati Asrama (1915) came from Tamil Nadu; G.D. Tendulkar, *Mahatma*, Volume I (Bombay, 1960).
8. H.F. Owen, "Organizing for the Rowlatt Satyagraha of 1919", in Ravinder Kumar (ed.), *Essays on Gandhian Politics: The Rowlatt Satyagraha of 1919* (Oxford, 1971).
9. *Hunter Commission Majority Report* (March 1920), Chapter IV, pp. 61-62.
10. *Hind Swaraj*, in M.K. Gandhi, *Collected Works*, Volume X.
11. Perhaps elsewhere, too; for we must remember that the Gandhian social ideal was derived in part from the Romantic critique of industrialism developed by mid-nineteenth century English writers. The value of such a critique has been emphasized by E.P. Thompson in *William Morris: Romantic to Revolutionary* (2nd edition, London, 1977). But it is significant that Gandhi's ideal was Ruskin, and not Morris who crossed the "river of fire" to "practical socialism".

12. For the nature and political significance of Gandhian rural constructive work, see Hitesh Sanyal, "Arambager Jatiyatabadi Andolan", *Anya Artha*, 1974-75, and "Dakshin Pashchim Banglay Jatiyatabadi Andolan", *Chaturanga*, 1977; Gyan Pandey; *Ascendancy of the Congress*, Chapter III; and Hardiman, *Peasant Nationalists*, Chapter 8.
13. The impact on Indian developments of the post-war world-wide upsurge, anti-capitalist in the developed countries and anti-imperialist in the colonies and semi-colonies, is difficult to document specifically but unrealistic to ignore. Indian soldiers coming home from distant lands must have carried with them something of the new revolutionary mood, and it is interesting that in an agrarian riot in March 1921 on the Rae Bareli-Pratapgarh border, the local leader, Brijpal Singh, was an ex-sepoy who, according to a police report, "obviously had great control over the crowd which was not lacking in a certain degree of military discipline". Siddiqi, *Agrarian Unrest*, p. 163.
14. Reading to the Secretary of State, 13 October 1921: Reading Collection (India Office Library).
15. Report by a CID Officer on the Kisan Sabha agitation, 7 January 1921, Home Political Deposit, February 1921, n 13.
16. Siddiqi, *op. cit.* Chapters III-IV.
17. That at least was G.D. Birla's impression after a talk with Gandhi, conveyed in a note to Purshottamdas Thakurdas which the latter sent to the Bombay Governor on 16 January 1941. Gandhi told Birla that he was worried about "the mentality of our young men... Communism appeals to youth, unfortunately". Birla's own comment is also interesting: "Was Satyagraha not a blessing in disguise? Was Gandhiji, by starting restricted Satyagraha, saving government from greater embarrassment and at the same time registering his own protest? Who knows?" Thakurdas Papers, File No.177.
18. Factory employment, in contrast, had increased from, 13,61,000 to 17,51,000 only between 1922 and 1939: Wadia and Merchant, *Our Economic Problem* (6th ed., Bombay, 1959). p. 355.

19. David Hardiman, *Peasant Nationalists,* Chapter 5.
20. R.L. Handa, *History of Freedom Struggle in Princely States* (New Delhi, 1968), pp. 116-117.
21. John R. Wood, "Rajkot: Indian Nationalism in the Princely. Context—the Rajkot Satyagraha of 1938-39" in Jeffrey (ed.), *People, Princes and Paramount Power.*
22. The Hyderabad movement for responsible government, for instance, was called off at Gandhi's insistence in December 1938, and the State Congress leader, Swami Ramanand Tirtha, later confessed: "We could not understand the propriety of this decision". Ramanand Thirtha, *Memoirs of Hyderabad Freedom Struggle* (Bombay, 1967), p. 107.
23. Brown, *Gandhi's Rise to Power,* p. 68.
24. Pouchepadass, "Champaran Satyagraha".
25. *Madras Forest Administration Report, 1921-22,* p. 30.
26. Viceroy to Secretary of State, 20 June 1921: Reading Collection.
27. Dhanagare, "Agrarian Conflict, Religion and Politics".
28. History of the Non-Cooperation and Khilafat Movements in Bengal—Government of Bengal, Political (Confidential), F.N. 395 S.N. 1-3 of 1924, pp. 13-14.
29. David Hardiman, *Peasant Nationalists,* pp. 195-96.
30. For a detailed account, see Tanika Sarkar, *National Movement and Popular Protest in Bengal, 1928-1934* (unpublished Ph.D. thesis, Delhi University, 1981), Chapter III.
31. Fortnightly Report from Bombay, second half of October 1930—Home Political 18/XI/1930. For more details about forest *satyagraha,* see my "Primitive Rebellion and Modern Nationalism: A Note on Forest Satyagraha in the Non-Cooperation and Civil Disobedience Movements", in K.N. Panikkar (ed.), *National and Left Movements in India* (Delhi, 1980).
32. See S. Sarkar, "Logic of Gandhian Nationalism: Civil Disobedience and the Gandhi Irwin Pact, 1930-31", *Indian Historical Review,* July 1976.
33. See Jawaharlal Nehru's reported comment at the crucial Working Committee session at Allahabad in April 1942 after

the collapse of the Cripps Mission: "It is Gandhiji's feeling that Japan and Germany will win. This feeling unconsciously governs his decision". *Congress Responsibility for the Disturbances* (Government of India, 1943), Appendix I.

34. *Ibid.*, Appendix IV.
35. Telegram to Churchill, 31 August 1942: N. Mansergh, (ed.), *Transfer of Power,* Volume II, p. 853.
36. Govind Sahai, *142 Rebellion* (Delhi, 1947). p. 96.
37. Text in *Congress Responsibility for the Disturbances,* Appendix VIII.
38. R.H. Niblett, *Congress Rebellion in Azamgarh* (Allahabad, 1957), pp. 29-31.
39. Henningham, *Protest and Control in North Bihar,* Chapter V.
40. Gyan Pandey, *Ascendancy of the Congress,* Chapters 6-7.
41. Tanika Sarkar, *National Movement and Popular Protest.*
42. Government of Bengal, Political (Confidential) F.N. 395 S.N. 1-3 of 1924, pp. 14-15.
43. R.P. Dutt's well-known comments on the Bardoli resolution of February 1922, emphasizing the condemnations of no-rent and assurances to landlords, remain difficult to refute, and it is interesting that Sitaramayya's *History of the Indian National Congress* does not give the text of this resolution while reprinting many less-important decisions. I have tried to explore the background and significance of the Gandhi-Irwin Pact in my "Logic of Gandhian Nationalism".
44. "In India we want no political strikes .... We must gain control over all the unruly and disturbing elements .... We seek not to destroy capital or capitalists, but to regulate the relations between capital and labour. We want to harness capital to our side. It would be folly to encourage sympathetic strikes". Gandhi, "The Lessons of Assam", *Young India,* 15 June 1921: *Collected Works,* Vol. 20, p. 228.
45. Gopal Krishna, "The Development of the Indian National Congress as a Mass Organization, 1918-1923", *Journal of Asian Studies,* May 1966.
46. Government of Bengal. Political (Confidential) F.N. 395, S.N. l-3 of 1924, p. 13.

47. Hardiman, *Peasant Nationalists,* p. 234; Pandey, *Ascendancy of the Congress,* Chapter V; Brian Stoddart, "The Structure of Congress Politics in Coastal Andhra", in D.A. Low, (ed.), *Congress and the Raj* (London 1977), pp. 121-22. The adverse consequences followed from the failure to regain confiscated peasant lands, and from the brake imposed in the interests of the truce on no-revenue and no-rent movements, at a time when the Depression was having its first major impact.
48. Tanika Sarkar, *National Movement and Popular Protest,* pp. 292-97.
49. Henningham, *Protest and Control in North Bihar,* Chapter V.
50. *Ibid.,* Chapter II.
51. Siddiqi, *Agrarian Unrest,* p. 157.
52. Tanika Sarkar, "A Study of Three Communal Riots in Bengal, 1930-31" in Mushirul Hasan (ed.), *Communal and Pan-Islamic Trends in Colonial India* (Delhi, 1981), p. 285.
53. Malkangiri Deputy *Tahsildar* to Agency Commissioner, 13 June 1923: M. Venkatarangaya (ed.), *Freedom Struggle in Andhra Pradesh,* Volume III (Hyderabad, 1965), p. 388.
54. D.O. from F.W. Stewart. Agency Commissioner, Narsapatam to Madras Chief Secretary, 26 September 1922: *Ibid.,* p. 373.
55. Madras Government Press Communique, 12 April 1924: *Ibid.,* p. 390.
56. Venkatarangaya, *op.cit.,* p. 90. For some more details about Sitarama Raju's movement, see my "Primitive Rebellion and Modern Nationalism", and Arnold, "Rebellious Hillmen".
57. Home Political F.N.104/1924 Note by 'E.H.F.' dated 19 March 1924.
58. K. Suresh Singh, *Colonial Transformation of Tribal Society in Middle India.*
59. Verrier Elwin, *Saora Fituris,* and Christoph Von Fürer-haimendorf, *Aboriginal Rebellions in the Deccan,* in *Man in India,* Rebellion Number, December 1945.
60. Stephen Henningham, "Agrarian Relations in North Bihar: Peasant Protest and the Darbhanga Raj, 1919-20", *Indian Economic and Social History Review,* 1979; Siddiqi, *Agrarian*

Unrest: Kapil Kumar, *Peasant Movements in Oudh, 1918-1922* (unpublished Ph.D. thesis, Meerut University, 1980).

60a. Thus Vidyanand's movement inspired sharecroppers in south-east Darbhangi to demand a change to cash rents (Stephen Henningham, "Agrarian Relations"). In the Awadh agrarian riots or January-March 1921, a Shah Naim Ata briefly proclaimed himself 'king of Salon' in Rae Bareli, crowds at Munshiganj in the same district were led by a Muslim *fakir* and a low caste Pasi *sadhu,* and a pretender 'Baba Ramchandra appeared in Fyzabad who tried to forcibly return *bedakhli* land to those evicted. Malcolm Hailey complained on 1 February 1921 that numerous *sadhus* "claim to be followers of Gandhi and speak in his name but their preaching is certainly not on the lines of Gandhi's ... as they advocate non-payment of rent and doctrines such as the land for the cultivator. There can be no doubt of course that they make the strongest appeal to the low castes and landless castes who...are told that a millennium in the shape of swaraj is coming through the intervention of Mahatma Gandhi". The relatively little-known Eka movement of 1921-22 was led by Madari Pasi. But despite such evidence of occasional low caste participation, it needs to be noted that of the 20 brought to trial after the Karhaiya bazaar clash with the police, 6 were Thakurs, 5 Brahmans, 5 Kurmis and only one Chamar. Siddiqi, *Agrarian Unrest,* pp. 150-70, 197-202.

61. Siddiqi, *ibid.,* p. 195. *The Indian Annual Register* (1929) records that "Baba Ramchandra (member of the UP Kisan Sabha)" opposed at the Calcutta session of the All Parties Conference an amendment to the draft Nehru Report, brought by Malaviya, guaranteeing "all titles to private and personal property".

62. Henningham, "Agarian Relations".

63. Gandhi bluntly declared in his "Instructions to UP Peasants" in March 1921: "We may not withold taxes from the government or rent from the landlord...it should be borne in mind that we want to turn zamindars into friends". *Young India,* 9 March 1921, reprinted in Gandhi, *Collected Works,*

Volume XIX pp. 419-20. See also Gyan Pandey, "Peasant Revolt and Indian Nationalism: The Peasant Movement in Awadh, 1919-1922", in *Subaltern Studies I.*

64. Walter Hauser, *Bihar Provincial Kisan Sabha, 1929-42,* (unpublished Ph.D. thesis, Chicago, 1961—NMML microfilm).
65. Tanika Sarkar, *National Movement and Popular Protest,* Chapters II, IV, V.
66. Kumar, "Bombay Textile Strike, 1919".
67. Vinay Behl, "Tata Iron and Steel Company-to Sramik Andolan, 1920-28", *Anya Artha,* 1975.
68. Thakurdas Papers, F.N. 42.
69. Rajnarayan Chandavarkar, "Workers Politics and the Mill Districts in Bombay between the Wars", in Baker, Johnson, Seal (ed.), *Power, Profit and Politics* (Cambridge 1981).
70. Sykes Papers and Halifax (Irwin) Collection at the India Office Library.
71. Tanika Sarkar, *National Movement and Popular Protest,* p. 142, citing an interview with Ranen Sen.

71a. In the first week of January 1922, for instance, there were 123 millhands among the 349 who had courted arrest, as against only 39 students. See Report of Calcutta Police Commissioner to Chief Secretary, Government of Bengal, 5 January, 1922: Government of Bengal, Political Department (Political Branch) F.N. 14 (21- 30)/1922.

71b. Telegram from Linlithgow to Amery, 21 August, 1942: *Transfer of Power* Vol. 2, p. 777.

72. As D.D. Kosambi pointed out in a brilliant piece of contemporary history-writing, "the glamour of jail and concentration camp served to wipe out the so-so record of the Congress ministries in office, thereby restoring the full popularity of the organization among the masses". See "The Bourgeoisie Comes of Age in India", *Science and Society,* 1946, (Reprinted in *Exasperating Essays,* Poona, n.d.).
73. J.B. Kripalani's analysis of post-war labour unrest, AICC FN G26/1946; V.B. Singh "Trade Union Movement", in Singh

(ed.), *Economic History of India, 1857-1956* (Bombay, 1965), p. 600.

74. For some details about the 1945-47 popular movements and Congress attitudes towards them, see my "Popular Movements, National Leadership, and the Coming of Freedom with Partition, 1945-47" (Paper presented at a Nehru Museum seminar, December 1980, and due for publication shortly in the *Economic and Political Weekly*).
75. Omvedt, *Cultural Revolt in a Colonial Society*.
76. B.R. Tomlinson, *The Indian National Congress and the Raj, 1929-1942* (Macmillan, 1976), Chapter III.
77. Siddiqi, *Agrarian Unrest*, pp. 114-17. The Baba Ramchandra Papers in the Nehru Museum contain some references to the Kurmi Kshatriya Sabha (I owe this information to Chandan Mitra).
78. Thus Gandhi rightly rebuked Narendra Dev on 2 August 1934 for forgetting to mention untouchability in the draft programme of the Congress Socialist Party (Tendulkar, *Mahatma*, Volume III, p. 344), and R.P. Dutt's *India Today* expressed an even viable confidence that caste would be "overcome, not by preaching and denunciation, but by the advance of modern industry and political democracy". (2nd edition, Bombay, 1947, p. 244).
79. The early twentieth century Nayar reformer K. Ramakrishna Pillai wrote the first Malayali biography of Karl Marx, E.M.S. Namboodiripad entered public life as a Nambudiri Welfare Association activist, A.K. Gopalan first become well-known as volunteer leader in the Guruvayur temple *satyagraha*, and militant Ezhaeva anti-Brahman movements led on through secularism towards Marxism. Robin Jeffrey, "Travancore: Status, class and the Growth of Radical Politics, 1860-1940", in Jeffrey (ed.), *People, Princes and Paramount Power*; E.M.S. Namboodiripad, *How I Became a Communist* (Trivandrum, 1976); A.K. Gopalan, *In the Cause of the People* (Madras, 1973).
80. Gyan Pandey, *Ascendancy of the Congress*, p. 202.

81. Telegrams of 15, 17 and 18 December 1921: Reading Collection.
82. Halifax (Irwin) Papers.
83. In a letter to Churchill dated 24 October 1944, Wavell argued that it would be impossible to hold India by force after the War. "We have had to negotiate with similar rebels before, e.g. De Valero and Zaghlul", and it would be wise to start negotiations before the inevitable post-war problems, which would create "a fertile field for agitation, unless we have previously diverted their [Congress] energies into some more profitable channel, i.e. into dealing with the administrative problems of India and into trying to solve the constitutional problem". Wavell, *The Viceroy's Journal* (Oxford, 1973), pp. 97- 98.
84. "Popular Movements, National Leadership, and the Coming of Freedom with Partition, 1945: 47".
85. Governor General (War Department) to Secretary of State, 30 November 1945: *Transfer of Power*, Volume VI, p. 572.
86. Wavell to George VI, 31 December 1945: *Transfer of Power*, Volume VI, p. 713.
87. G.D. Birla to Henderson, 6 December 1945: *Ibid.*, p. 615.
88. Governor Colville of Bombay to Wavell, 27 February 1946: *Ibid.*, pp. 1081-82.
89. *Viceroy's Journal*, p. 329.
90. Note by N.P.A. Smith, Director, Intelligence Bureau, Home Department, 9 August 1946; Home Political (Internal), 12/7/46. Wavell had already informed Pethick Lawrence on 31 July, with a countrywide postal strike still on and two days after a massive Calcutta *bundh*, that the Congress would have to be asked to form the Interim Government on their own. "If Congress will take responsibility they will realize that firm control of unruly elements is necessary and they may put down the Communists and try to curb their own left wing. Also I should hope to keep them so busy with administration that they had much less time for politics". Mansergh, *Transfer of Power*, Volume VIII, pp. 154-55.

91. Thus *khadi,* salt, Harijan welfare, and other aspects of Gandhian rural constructive work provided no solutions to basic problems of agrarian relations, but they could bring some limited but real benefits, instilling both self-confidence and faith in a leadership which was seen to be achieving something concrete. See articles by Hitesh Sanyal cited in f.n. 162; David Hardiman, *Peasant Nationalists,* Chapter 8.
92. Antonio Gramsci, "Notes on Italian History", in Hoare and Smith (ed.), *Selections from Prison Notebooks* (New York, 1971), p. 59.
93. Subhas Bose in a letter to Nehru on 28 March 1939 offered the following unkind but probably not too unjust characterization of Jawaharlal's role in Working Committee meetings: "You would generally hold forth for hours together and then succumb at the end. Sardar Patel and others had a clever technique for dealing with you. They would let you talk and talk and they would ultimately finish up by asking you to draft *their* resolution. Once you were allowed to draft the resolution, you would feel happy, no matter whose resolution it was. Rarely have I found you sticking to your point till the last". *A Bunch of Old Letters* (Asia, 1958), p. 340. Bose did not have Nehru's personal loyalty to Gandhi, but it has to be added that his own performance was really no better. He chose to break on the issue of his own re-election as President, not on matters of principle like the Bombay Trade Disputes Bill or the increasingly anti-Kisan Sabha stance of Congress ministries.
94. Benthall's diaries for 1928-33 records fascinating details about the way in which an initially sharp conflict with G.D. Birla over jute trading interests gradually gave way to increasing cooperation. In a note written after 1947, Benthall recalled with some pride that though he had been known at one time as " 'Bengali Sahib' among certain of the die-hard elements, looking back I have no doubt that the policy followed by the leaders of British business throughout this anxious time was right, for the responsible line we took over the 20 years

leading up to Independence, capped of course by the willingness of HMG's Government to grant that independence, prepared the way for the fair manner in which the Congress Government dealt with us when they came into power". Benthall Papers, Cambridge South Asia Study Centre, Box No. XI and XII.

95. During a visit to Calcutta in May 1947, for instance, Gandhi advised workers of a Birla-owned mill to end their strike, warning "the mill-hands against being used as tools for the accentuation of the class war or in furtherance of certain ideologies". Pyarelal, *Mahatma Gandhi: The Last Phase,* Volume II (Allahabad, 1958), p. 177.

96. For more details, see my "Logic of Gandhian Nationalism" and *Popular Movements;* Basudev Chatterji, "Business and Politics in the 1930s: Lancashire and the Making of the Indo-British Trade Agreement, 1939", and Claude Markovits, "Indian Business and the Congress Provincial Government, 1937- 39" both in *Power, Profit and Politics.*

96a. Bipan Chandra, "The Indian Capitalist Class and Imperialism before 1947" in his *Nationalism and Colonialism in Modern India* (New Delhi, 1979), p. 145. For an alternative view emphasizing the complexities and internal divisions within Indian business groups, see articles by Chatterji and Markovits cited in the previous footnote.

97. Shanin, *The Awkward Class;* for some of the political consequences, see also Moshe Lewin, *Russian Peasants and Soviet Power* (London, 1968).

98. Utsa Patnaik, "Class Differentiation within the Peasantry: An Approach to Analysis of Indian Agriculture" *Economic and Political Weekly,* 25 September 1976. The existence from pre-colonial times of a large class of low-caste landless labour also makes Jainus Banaji's attempt to apply Marx's distinction between 'formal' and 'real' subsumption of hour to capital rather difficult, for in a sense 'formal subsumption' abstracted from technical transformation may go back very far in time. J. Banaji, "Capitalist Domination and the Small Peasantry:

Deccan Districts in the Late 19th Century", *Economic and Political Weekly*, Special Number, August 1977.

99. Hardiman's thesis (available in typescript at the Nehru Museum), article in *Congress and the Raj*, and book offer rather different approaches to this problem; see also Neil Charlesworth, "The 'Middle Peasant Thesis' and the Roots of Rural Agitation in India, 1914-47" (*Journal* of *Peasant Studies*, April 1980), and David Hardiman, "Roots of Rural Agitation in India, 1914-47: A Rejoinder to Charlesworth" (*Ibid*., April 1981).
100. D.A. Low, Introduction to *Congress and the Raj.*
101. Hitesh Sanyal pointed out in his "Arambager Jatiyatabadi Andolan", that only 9 per cent of the 371 jailed for political activities in Arambagh during 1930-42, about whom data is available, had more than 15 *bighas* (5 acres) of land.
102. David Hardiman, "The Crisis of the Lesser Patidars: Peasant Agitation in Kheda District, 1917-34", in *Congress and the Raj.*
103. D.A. Washbrook, *Emergence of Provincial Politics: Madras Presidency, 1870-1920* (Cambridge, 1976), Chapter 3.
104. Hardiman, "The Crisis of the Lesser Patidars".
105. H.R. Nevili (ed.), *Rae Bareli District Gazetter* (Lucknow, 1923), pp. 25-28, 46-48.
106. *Settlement Report, Pratapgarh, 1896*, pp. ii, 50, 58-9.
107. *Settlement Report, Pratapgarh, 1930*, p. 2. Alok Sheel has recently drawn pointed attention to the danger of using the "rhetoric of absolute impoverishment of all sections" under British rule as a facile explanation for Gandhian or Kisan movements in his very impressive unpublished M.Phil. dissertation, *The Congress and the Raiyat : A Study of Three Agrarian Movements, 1928-40* (JNU, 1981).
108. David Hardiman, "Roots of Rural Agitation in India".
109. "The government wants to divide you and the shahukar, but for you, your shahukar is everything ....It is just like saying to a *pativrata* that she should change her husband". *Satyagraha Patrika*, 18 March and 8 April 1928, cited in Ghanshyam Shah, "Traditional Society and Political Mobilization: The

Experience of Bardoli Satyagraha", *Contributions to Indian Sociology*, New Series, No. 11, 1974.

110. Jan Breman described the *hali* system attaching Dublas to Anavil Brahmans as "a form of unfree labour, complicated and mitigated by a relation of patronage". *Patronage and Exploitation: Changing Agrarian Relations in South Gujarat, India* (California, 1974), p. 21.
111. Ghanshyam Shah, *op. cit.*
112. David Hardiman, *Peasant Nationalists*, pp. 111-12.
113. Pyarelal, *Mahatma Gandhi : The Last Phase*, Volume II, pp. 24-25.
114. *Ibid.*, pp. 645-59.
115. *Ibid.*, Appendix I
116. *Ibid.*, p. 119. Pyarelal puts this passage in italics.
117. *Indian Annual Register*, 1936.
118. P.C. Joshi, *For the Final Bid for Power* (Bombay, 1945), p. 118.
119. P. Sundarayya, *Telengana People's Struggle and its Lessons* (Calcutta, 1972), p. 124. The initial ceiling decided on had been even higher, 500 acres.
120. The Shertalai-Alleppey-Ambalapuzha area was marked by a close proximity of small-town industries (like coir factories) with agricultural occupations and Alleppey workers, fishermen and Kuttanad farm labourers fought side by side at Punnapra Vayalar. K.C. George, *Immortal, Punnapra-Vayalar* (New Delhi, 1975); R. Jeffrey, "A Sanctified Label: Congress in Travancore Politics, 1938-48", in *Congress and the Raj*.
121. Ranajit Guha's forthcoming book on elementary forms of peasant struggle promises to be a pathbreaker in this direction. I take this opportunity to acknowledge my debt to him, particularly for a stimulating all-night discussion I was privileged to have with him in Brighton in 1977.
122. G. Rude, "The Pre-Industrial 'Crowd'", in *Paris and London in the 18th Century: Studies in Popular Protest* (Fontana, 1970), referring to popular actions taken in the name of a distant superior or king, as well as to followers out running leaders

123. Thus there is the story of the Jat Tejaji in Rajasthan honoured for having offered himself to be bitten by a snake to stop it from drinking up the milk of a cow belonging to a Brahman, Crooke and Enthoven, *Religion and Folklore of Northern India*, p. 165.
124. "Story of Bhar Bitna", in P.C. Roy Chaudhuri, *Folk Tales of Bihar* (Sahitya Akademi, 1968).
125. "The Farmer and the Moneylender", in Flora Steel, *Folktales of Punjab* (a Vikas reprint, 1974, of a nineteenth century collection). I am grateful to Dr. Gyan Pandey for drawing my attention to this story.

4

Conclusion

Despite the crucial importance of popular movements .and pressures from below throughout the late-colonial period, the leadership in the anti-imperialist struggle thus remained with relatively privileged groups in city and countryside alike. The resultant complex and contradictory pattern, epitomized by the nature of the August 1947 'transfer of power', can perhaps be best analyzed, I would like to suggest in conclusion, through Gramsci's concept of 'passive revolution'.

Reacting against the once-common 'sectarian' tendency to see only compromise and betrayal in the Gandhian leadership and a false freedom in August 1947, a trend has developed in recent years to emphasize rather the positive aspects of that leadership. The national bourgeoisie, we are told, achieved through Gandhi a genuine 'hegemony' over the anti-imperialist movement. It is important in this context, however, to remember that Gramsci used the concept of hegemony in two quite distinct senses. There is the classic 'Jacobin' model of successful and thorough going bourgeois revolution based on mobilization of the peasantry and total destruction of feudalism, as well as the very different case of mid-nineteenth century Italy, where fundamental agrarian change remained a *revoluzione mancata* as peasant aspirations were sacrificed through the formation of a bloc between

Northern industrialists and Southern landlords, and full scale capitalist transformation proved very difficult to achieve. In the second case, there was a much more partial or limited 'hegemony', confined mainly to the political level and achieved through the process of *transformism* which Gramsci explicitly relates to his concept of passive revolution—'passive' not in the sense of popular forces being inactive or unimportant, but because attainment of political independence and unity was successfully detached by the leading bourgeois group (the Moderates headed by Cavour) from radical social change. A further consequence was the perpetuation and sharpening of regional disparities, the North flourishing at the cost of the South—modern Italy's persistent *questione meridionale.* Historical parallals can never be exact, but some of the similarities do appear almost uncanny—and it is interesting that Gramsci in 1933 made a passing reference to Gandhism as a "naive theorization of the 'passive revolution' with religious overtones".[1]

Analogies apart, the value of the 'passive revolution' concept lies in its theoretical comprehension of two types of relative failure. If popular forces failed to achieve an alternative hegemony, the dependent bourgeoisie of colonial India on the whole revealed in its behaviour at best the "modest egoism" which Marx had found typical of the pre-1848 German burgher estate, and not the world-transforming revolutionary zeal of the French bourgeoisie of 1789.[2] The inhibiting factors here included relations of dependence and collaboration with foreign rule and British capital, close connections with pre-capitalist forms of exploitation of the small producer through rent, usury and trade (which under colonial conditions often remained so much more profitable than productive investment in industry or agriculture), fear of an already fairly militant working class, as well as the lack of cultural hegemony in so far as there was little permeation of modern bourgeois values throughout society. 'Modernism' in our country was largely confined to a 'middle class' with little roots in production, while the mental world of the bulk of Indian traders, industrialists, or rich peasants remained bound to pre-modern caste and religious loyalties. There was thus no breakthrough from the 'economic-corporative', to the 'hegemonic' phase of bourgeois class development: a leap associated by Gramsci with the development of an "organic intelligentsia"'. This, I presume, is the important point being made by Ranajit Guha when he defines as

> *the central problematic of the historiography of colonial India...* the study of this *historic failure of the nation to come to its own,* a failure due to the inadequacy of the bourgeoisie as well as of the working class to lead it into a decisive victory over colonialism and a bourgeois-democratic revolution of either the classic nineteenth century type under the hegemony of the bourgeoisie or a more modern type under the hegemony of workers and peasants...[3]

It would be interesting to speculate as to whether 'passive revolution' has continued in post-independence India, and whether the failure of the Left to build any alternative hegemony is related to the lack of the flexibility and sophistication necessary to counter a ruling class, skilled in moving to some extent with the times and an old hand at appropriating radical or populist slogans. But that would be going beyond the scope of this paper, and I have already presumed far too much on your time and patience.

NOTES

1. Gramsci, *Selections from Prison Notebooks,* pp. 59, 107 and *passim.*
2. Karl Marx, *Introduction to a Contribution to the Critique* of *Hegel's Philosophy of Right* (1844),—in Karl Marx, *Early Writings* (London, 1975), p. 255.
3. Ranajit Guha, "On Some Aspects of the Historiography of Colonial India". *Subaltern Studies I,* p. 7 (Guha's italics).